GLENCOE

Hands-On Health

Creative Teaching Strategies

Deborah L. Tackmann, B.S., M.E.P.D.

Health Education Instructor
North High School
Eau Claire, Wisconsin

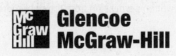

Glencoe McGraw-Hill

New York, New York   Columbus, Ohio   Woodland Hills, California   Peoria, Illinois

Acknowledgements

The author and editors would like to thank the following educators who helped create some of the activities in this booklet:

Gretchen Beckstrom, Activity 2, "A Letter to Yourself."

Dr. Penny Lyter, Activity 13, "Rate Your Snack Foods," Activity 14, "Name That Food," Activity 15, "Fat on a Bun."

Melissa Arndt, Activity 39, "Sexual Health Contract."

Activities 11, "Cups of Calcium" and 12, "Rubber Bones" were adapted with permission from the Western Dairy Council, 12000 N. Washington, Suite 200, Thornton, CO 80241.

Cover Photo Credits

(left to right) Digital Stock Corporation; Aaron Haupt; Jim Cummins/FPG International LLC; Anthony Redpath, Jim Ericson/The Stock Market; FPG International LLC, VCG

 Glencoe

The *McGraw-Hill* Companies

Send all inquiries to:
Glencoe/McGraw-Hill
21600 Oxnard Street, Suite 500
Woodland Hills, California 91367

ISBN 0-07-823786-6 Hands-On Health: Creative Teaching Strategies

Printed in the United States of America.

    9 10 11 12 13 14 15   045   12 11 10 09 08 07

Table of Contents

Substance Abuse and Alcohol

Disease Prevention

Community Health

Human Sexuality and Abstinence

STDs, HIV, and AIDS

First Aid

Consumer Education

Introduction

The *Hands-On Health: Creative Teaching Strategies* booklet presents a variety of unique, motivating hands-on activities designed specifically to facilitate student thinking and involvement in the learning process. The activities and strategies in this booklet are arranged according to health content area, to help you find and select the activities that will best support any aspect of your health curriculum.

What Are Hands-On Activities?

Hands-on activities take students out—out of their books, often out of their seats, and sometimes out of the classroom. More significantly, hands-on activities take students out of their familiar avenues of thinking. These activities are intended to make students active participants in their own education.

Why Use Hands-On Activities?

There is a big difference between passive learning and active learning. Hands-on activities are the most effective means of helping students learn and remember. Students, like the rest of us, tend to recall only 10 percent of what they read. They may recall 20 percent of what they hear and 30 percent of what they see. When students become more involved by participating in a discussion or by giving a talk on a particular subject, their rate of recall rises to 70 percent. The most impressive rate of recall occurs when students are most fully involved; that is, when they participate in a dramatic presentation, simulate a real experience, or actually do "the real thing."

This high rate of recall can enable students to make safe, respectful, and healthy lifestyle decisions, both now and in the years ahead. How can you involve students more fully in the learning process? While there are many aspects to this involvement, you will find that integrating hands-on activities into the classroom routine can play an important role.

Getting Started

The hands-on teaching strategies in this booklet are intended to inspire both you and your students. You will probably want to look through the booklet and find the activities that best suit your students' needs and your curriculum.

The first section includes several general Classroom Management Strategies that can be used in a variety of ways to open the class period, to introduce a lesson or unit, and to encourage students to participate and become actively involved throughout the lessons. You might find, for instance, that the "Beach Ball" strategy helps students who are hesitant to join in during class discussions, or that "Exchange Papers" makes efficient use of class time and also encourages students to get to know one another.

Presentation

Preparation and presentation are key elements for you to consider as you use these strategies in your classroom. First you will find the overall Objective stated for each strategy. Teacher Notes give you helpful information when using the activity, describe expected student outcomes, and provide important tips on being sensitive to the needs and issues of your particular classroom. Some of the activities include a blackline master that would work well as an overhead transparency. You can create transparencies easily using a copy machine and transparency paper that is readily available in office supply stores.

An estimate of time is listed to give you an idea of how long it takes to present an activity, but keep in mind that you and your students may wish to vary this estimated time depending on your situation. A list of materials not commonly found in the classroom is provided to help you in pre-class preparation and assure that the activity goes smoothly.

Cooperative Learning

Many of the activities involve students working with partners or in cooperative groups. Unless your students have extensive experience working in cooperative learning groups, you may choose to assign students to these partnerships or groups. It is important that these pairings or groupings reflect the diversity of real life—they should be mixed socially, ethnically, by gender, and by learning abilities.

In addition, you will want to remind students of the three basic rules of cooperative learning: Stay with your group. Ask a question of the teacher only after all group members agree that no one in the group has the answer. Offer feedback on ideas; avoid criticizing people.

Health for Life

You are encouraged to adapt the teaching strategies provided here as your own. Edit them, expand them, revise them. Listen to suggestions from your colleagues, your friends, and your students. Learning about health is a lifelong process, and learning about teaching health should be, too. *Hands-On Health: Creative Teaching Strategies* can be one of your essential learning tools. Have fun with your students and get them working hands-on with their health education!

Classroom Management Strategies

Classroom Management Strategies

Beach Ball

OBJECTIVE   To review facts or vocabulary terms

STRATEGY   As you call a student's name, toss a beach ball (or another soft object, such as a beanbag) to that student. When the student catches the ball, ask a short review question or give the definition of a vocabulary term. Have the student answer the question or name the vocabulary term while tossing the ball back to you.

Trivia Question

OBJECTIVE   To review facts already presented or to stimulate interest in the day's lesson

STRATEGY   Before class, write a trivia question on the board. You may want to base this question on information in a recent lesson or on information that will be covered in the day's reading and discussion. Have students write down their answers and hand them to you before the bell rings. Reward each correct answer (as with a Bonus Buck, page xi), but explain that credit can be given only to students who turn in a correct answer *and* are ready for class when the bell rings. Ask students not to discuss the questions and their answers until the following class meeting, when you may want to write the answer on the board.

Exchange Papers

OBJECTIVE   To develop a positive classroom environment

STRATEGY   When students correct assignments in class, have them exchange papers with different classmates and encourage them to learn more about their peers. For example, ask students to find and exchange papers with someone with whom they have one of the following in common:

- color of eyes or hair
- color of socks or shoes
- month of birth
- city, state, or country of birth
- number of siblings

Vary your suggestions to encourage students to get to know all their classmates.

Mental Outburst

OBJECTIVE   To review facts or vocabulary terms

STRATEGY   Prepare several different cards with groups of facts or vocabulary terms. At the top of each card, write the name of a general category. Then list ten words or phrases that fit the category. Here is a sample card:

CATEGORY: SIGNS OF SUICIDE	
hopelessness	poor hygiene
lack of energy	increased risk taking
withdrawal from friends	rebellious behavior
giving away possessions	drugs and alcohol use
drop in grades	violent actions

Laminate the cards so students can mark on them with transparency markers and then wipe the cards clean.

Use the cards for review games. Have students form groups, and give one member of each group one of the cards. The student with the card reads the category title aloud and does not show the card to anyone else. The other group members call out words or phrases that fit the category, trying to match those on the card. The student with the card checks off each item the others identify correctly. Call time for all groups after one minute (or a period you consider appropriate for your students and the cards you have prepared). If students want to keep score, have the members of each group record the number of checkmarks they got on that card. Then have group members wipe their cards clean and exchange cards with another group.

Continue playing until each group has used every card.

What's In a Name?

OBJECTIVE   To review and sort vocabulary terms related to a given topic

STRATEGY   List all the important vocabulary terms for a particular unit. (You may have as many as 50 terms, for example.) Print each term on a separate slip of paper to make a complete set of terms; photocopy or rewrite the terms on more slips of paper to make additional sets. You should have enough sets of terms so that each group of three or four students has its own set.

Have students form small groups, and give each group a complete set of terms, a large piece of poster board, and 12 stick-on notes. Instruct the members of each group to read all the terms and then to sort the terms into related categories. They should agree on at least three and no more than six categories. If students are unsure about the meanings of any words, they should discuss their ideas and consult a textbook or other source of information if necessary. Have students arrange the word groups on the poster board, using a stick-on note to label each group.

When students have completed this grouping, they go on to Round 2. The same students work together to sort the same terms into completely new categories. Again, they should have no fewer than three and no more than six categories of terms, and they should use stick-on notes to label the new word groups.

When all the groups have sorted the terms into two completely different categories, help the whole class discuss the activity and review any terms that caused special problems.

Health Bonus Bucks

OBJECTIVE   To encourage participation and to help develop a positive classroom environment

STRATEGY   Photocopy the Health Bonus Bucks (page xi) onto green paper if possible, and cut them apart. Keep a supply of Bonus Bucks ready to pass out as motivators for correct responses, exceptional behavior, etc.

Explain to students how they can use their Bonus Bucks. For example, you may want to let students use a Bonus Buck to "buy" a hall pass, the right to borrow a pencil for a class period, a sheet of notebook paper, and/or an extra point on a worksheet or test.

Health
and
Wellness

Three Wishes

OBJECTIVE To recognize the importance of wellness and the impact that health can have on students' goals for the future

TEACHER NOTES This activity involves a letter informing students that they are suffering from an incurable terminal disease. You may want to consider the situations of individual students and their families before reading the letter.

TIME 15–20 minutes

SUPPLIES
- writing paper for each student
- pen or pencil for each student
- stick (decorated or colorful, if possible) to serve as a "magic wand"
- copy of Activity 1, "Letter from a Doctor" (page 4)
- envelope for each student (optional)

STEPS

1. Display your "magic wand" and explain that it enables you to grant three wishes to every student.

2. Tell students that the magic from this wand will last for only the next 30 seconds, and within that time they should write down their three wishes. (Explain that they may not wish for additional wishes.)

3. Encourage students to share and discuss their wishes with a partner. Follow with a brief class discussion. List their wishes on the board.

4. Take out the "Letter from a Doctor." Tell the class: Imagine that you have just received this letter and it is addressed to you.

5. Read the letter aloud to the students. Let them share their reactions. Ask: How does this news change your ideas about your three wishes?

6. Have students review their three wishes and cross out those that would no longer have the same value if they were terminally ill.

FOLLOW-UP

Help students discuss the importance of good health and wellness. Encourage them to explore how their own lifestyle decisions can help determine the level of their own wellness, both now and in the future.

Letter from a Doctor

Dear _____,

    I regret that I have bad news for you. As you recall, we ran a number of medical tests last week. The results of those tests have been returned to me. Unfortunately, they confirm that you have a terminal disease. I have consulted a number of experts, and all agree that there is no cure or treatment for your disease. You can expect to live for another two weeks or, at most, two months.

    I am very sorry.

Yours sincerely,

L. L. Lessen

L. L. Lessen, M.D.

Letter to Yourself

OBJECTIVE   To help students assess their personal attitudes toward health-related issues and behaviors

TEACHER NOTES   This activity involves a personal evaluation of attitudes and lifestyle choices. Assure students that their letters are for their personal use only and will remain confidential. You will keep them sealed and return them so students may review them at the end of the semester or academic year.

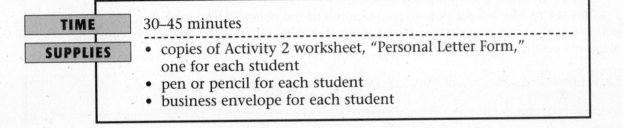

TIME	30–45 minutes
SUPPLIES	• copies of Activity 2 worksheet, "Personal Letter Form," one for each student • pen or pencil for each student • business envelope for each student

STEPS

1. Explain that students are going to write letters to very special people: themselves. In these letters, they should be open and honest about their own ideas, beliefs, and actions. Assure students that the letters they write will not be read by you or anyone else.

2. Distribute copies of the worksheet and have students complete the letters, either in class or as homework.

3. After students complete their letters, have them address the envelopes to themselves. In the upper right corner, where the stamp would go, have them write the year they will graduate from high school. Students should then place their letters inside the envelopes and seal them.

4. Collect the envelopes, alphabetize them by last name, and place them in a box. Tell students that throughout the course they will have opportunities to review, add to, or change their letters.

5. Within the context of the course, periodically give students a chance to review and edit their letters. You may choose to do this after each health unit (i.e., tobacco or sexuality).

FOLLOW-UP

Guide students in discussing what they learned by writing these letters. Encourage volunteers to share some of their responses.

To show how attitudes and lifestyle behaviors may change as a person grows, you might arrange for students in an earlier grade to write similar letters as part of a health class, place them in envelopes, and have the letters follow those students on to their high school health class, where they would compare and contrast their sixth-grade and ninth-grade letters.

Name _____ Date _____ Class Period _____

Personal Letter Form

Directions: Fill in the lines below to create a letter to yourself that you can review later.

_____
(date)

Dear _____ ,

    This seems like a good time to record some of my beliefs, ideas, and choices. I want you to know about my attitudes toward certain health-related issues and my commitment to specific lifestyles.

This is how I describe my physical appearance: (height, weight, hairstyle, etc.)

_____

_____

This is how I see myself: (friendly, outgoing, quiet, etc.)

_____

_____

This is what I like to do in my spare time: (hobbies, activities, etc.)

_____

_____

These are my three best friends:

_____

_____

The roles my peers have in influencing the decisions I make are:

_____

_____

These are my favorite thing(s) to eat:

_____

_____

Activity (2) continued

This is the kind of music I enjoy listening to, and these are my favorite songs:

_____

_____

My favorite TV show and favorite movie are:

_____

_____

This is what I want to accomplish in the next four years:

_____

_____

These are two qualities I like about myself:

_____

_____

I would like to change these two qualities about myself:

_____

_____

These are my views on tobacco:

_____

_____

These are my views on alcohol:

_____

_____

These are my views on marijuana use:

_____

_____

This is my view on being sexually abstinent before marriage:

_____

_____

The person who has had the most influence on my life is: (tell why)

_____

_____

If I could make a change to improve the quality of my present life and health, it would be:

_____

_____

(Add any other comments you'd like to make here.)

_____

_____

    This is what I am thinking and feeling right now. If I make any important changes, I'll get back to you.

                   Your best friend,

                   _____
                   sign your name here

Mental and
Emotional Health

First Aid for Avoiding Conflict

OBJECTIVE   To recognize the impact that negative words and actions may have on a person's wellness

TEACHER NOTES   In scheduling this activity, keep in mind that it begins in one class meeting and must be continued in the next class meeting.

| TIME | • 10 minutes in one class meeting
• 20–30 minutes in the following class meeting |
| SUPPLIES | adhesive bandages, one for each student |

STEPS

1. Have students think about what kinds of negative words or actions they have seen at school, on the news, in music, on television, or in the movies. List those ideas on the board.

2. Next, guide students in discussing their own experiences with negative words and actions. What are some examples? What are their effects?

3. After a brief discussion, distribute the adhesive bandages. Have each student unwrap the bandage and apply it to the back of his or her dominant hand.

4. Ask students how long it took them to unwrap the bandage and put it on. A typical response is 10 to 15 seconds. Tell students that while they were putting on their bandages, a person somewhere in the United States was being battered, harassed, or purposely hurt. This happens every 10 to 15 seconds in our country! Discuss the impact that violent behavior has on a person's health. Ask: What strategies can you suggest to stop the violence?

5. Have students keep their bandages on until the next class meeting (or for at least 24 hours). Have them use the bandage as a constant reminder to use only positive words and actions.

6. At the next class meeting, have students discuss their experiences in using positive words and actions. In which situations was this most difficult? How did others respond to their positive behaviors? What strategies did they use to remain positive? How did they feel about using this positive approach?

7. Guide the class in discussing the relationship between negative words and physical violence. Ask students to suggest strategies that can be used, or that they have used in the last 24 hours, to reduce violence in their school and their community; list specific suggestions on the board.

FOLLOW-UP

Have students form cooperative learning groups. Ask the members of each group to select from the list on the board one strategy for reducing violence. Then have group members develop and share with the rest of the class a plan for implementing that strategy.

Activity 4

Personal Stress Buster

OBJECTIVE   To identify personal stressors, the impact that stress has on a person's wellness, and effective ways to manage or reduce stress

TEACHER NOTES   This activity gives you an opportunity to assess students' understanding of their own stressors and strategies for managing stress. Be sure to consider students' privacy when doing this activity.

TIME   20 minutes, plus time for individual conferences where necessary

SUPPLIES
- copies of Activity 4 worksheet, "Stress Test," one for each student
- pen or pencil for each student

STEPS

1. Distribute copies of Activity 4 worksheet, and go over the directions with students. Emphasize the importance of identifying specific stressors. As an example, explain that a *math test tomorrow* is a more specific stressor than *schoolwork.*

2. Let students work privately to complete their own worksheets.

3. Collect and read the worksheets. Evaluate each student's ability to identify and manage the stressors in his or her life. Arrange to talk privately with any student who appears to be having problems identifying or managing stress. In some cases, you may want to talk with the student's parents or ask a school counselor to intervene.

FOLLOW-UP

After two or three weeks, ask students to recall the healthy strategies they identified for coping with stress. Have them describe, either in group discussion or in short compositions, their own evaluations of the success of those strategies.

Name _____ Date _____ Class Period _____

Stress Test

Directions: Identify two specific stressors in your life. Write a word or phrase to identify each stressor on one of the lines below.

_____ — (**ME**) — _____

1. Choose one of the stressors you named and answer the following questions.

   a. What details help explain this stressor? _____

   _____

   _____

   b. How do you feel about this stressor? _____

   _____

   _____

   c. Why do you feel stress in response to this person, thing, event, or situation? _____

   _____

   _____

   d. What unsuccessful efforts have you made to manage this stressor? _____

   _____

   _____

2. List three specific strategies you can use to manage or cope with the stressor.

   a. _____

   b. _____

   c. _____

A Heavy Load

OBJECTIVE   To identify stressors that teens are often expected to manage, and to understand the impact that unmanaged stress can have on a person's overall wellness

TEACHER NOTES   This activity helps students recognize specific stressors in the lives of many teens. Depending on your students' experiences, you may want to modify the letter in this activity. Retitle the stressor books as necessary to fit the situation in your modified letter.

TIME   20–30 minutes

SUPPLIES
- copy of Activity 5 worksheet, "Letter from a Student"
- large backpack
- 8 textbooks of varying sizes and weights

Cover each book with plain paper. Use a black marker to label each book with the name of a common stressor:

Separated Parents	Alcoholism
Verbal Abuse	Negative Peer Pressure
Low Self-Esteem	Eating Disorder
Trouble in School	Suicidal Thoughts

STEPS

1. Tell students that you have received a letter from a student in one of your other classes asking for help.

2. Read the letter aloud to the class. Ask students to share their reactions.

3. Have a volunteer come forward to represent the student in the letter and put on the empty backpack.

4. Read the letter again, and have the class identify stressors in the letter that the teen is trying to confront. As each stressor is identified, have one student come up, choose the book representing that stressor, and place it in the backpack.

5. When the backpack is full of all eight textbooks, ask the volunteer how he or she feels carrying this heavy load.

6. Have students discuss their responses to these questions: How do you think carrying this heavy backpack, hour after hour and day after day, would affect any student's wellness? What can the volunteer do to lighten the load in this backpack? What can the letter writer do to lighten the load of stressors?

7. Guide students in discussing strategies they can use to assure that their own "backpacks" of stressors do not become unmanageable. Help students recognize how they can manage stress.

FOLLOW-UP

Let students meet in groups to brainstorm specific ways in which the letter writer might be helped.

Letter from a Student

Dear Teacher,

    I need your help! You said that we could always come and talk to you if we were having problems, and I am definitely having problems.

    My parents argue constantly and my mom is threatening to leave. Every day when I get home, someone yells at me about something. I feel like I can't do anything right. I didn't study for my history test and I know my grades are just getting worse and worse.

    My aunt drinks a lot and sometimes she gets sick so my mom goes over to take care of her. Besides putting up with my dad's yelling, I have to clean the house, cook dinner, do the laundry, and take care of my little brothers almost every night. I am going crazy!

    I find myself hanging out with a group of kids who party and drink a lot. Sometimes I think that if I can just escape my life for a little while, I'll be able to survive, and maybe pot or alcohol can do that for me, but it scares me to think I might become like my aunt.

    I thought that if I lost weight, my friends would like me better and maybe a certain boy would pay attention to me. I didn't eat for three days. Then I passed out in the girls' bathroom. That really scared me, too!

    I just don't know what to do. I feel so alone, and I wonder if anyone cares about me at all. Maybe the world would be better off without me.

    If you have the time, could you please talk with me? I really need help!

                      A Student in Your Fourth-Period Class

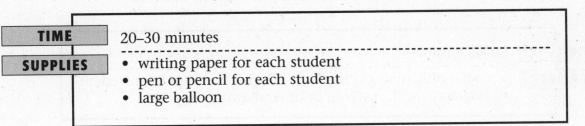

Stress Balloon

OBJECTIVE　　To identify personal stressors and to recognize the impact stress can have on wellness

TEACHER NOTES　　This activity helps students visualize the damaging effects stress can have on wellness.

TIME	20–30 minutes
SUPPLIES	• writing paper for each student • pen or pencil for each student • large balloon

STEPS

1. Have students draw a large circle in the middle of their papers, leaving space around the outside of the circle. Inside this circle, have them list the stressors in their lives.

2. In a general discussion, ask students to identify stressors that teens encounter every day. Every time a student identifies a common stressor, blow a puff of air into the balloon. Point out that the air in the balloon is like stress in students' lives.

3. When the balloon is nearly full, ask students what will happen if you continue to blow air into it. Then ask them to predict what might happen to a person's physical, emotional, social, and intellectual wellness if stress goes unmanaged.

4. Ask students to identify effective, healthy strategies for managing stress. You may want to suggest some examples: take a walk, talk to someone about your feelings, or set clear priorities. Every time a student identifies a healthy strategy, let a puff of air out of the balloon.

5. Then challenge students to consider the personal stressors they noted inside the circles on their papers. Have students draw arrows pointing to the circle, and have students identify strategies that can be effectively used to manage stress in their lives. Tell them to write these "stress busters" along the arrows.

FOLLOW-UP

Ask volunteers to plan, practice, and then present to the class skits about teens coping with stress.

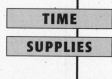
Coat of Arms

OBJECTIVE To identify personal traits, accomplishments, and goals, and to be able to communicate these to others

TEACHER NOTES Students can use this activity to examine their personal values and intentions. Before you assign the worksheet, decide whether students will turn them in or keep their responses private.

TIME 30–45 minutes

- -

SUPPLIES
- copies of Activity 7, "My Coat of Arms," one for each student
- colored pencils, markers, or other drawing supplies

STEPS

1. Distribute the worksheet and review the instructions with students.

2. Have students work independently to complete their coats of arms.

3. After students have completed their coats of arms, direct them to form groups of four or five and take turns showing and describing their coats of arms with classmates. You as the teacher may wish to create a coat of arms yourself and demonstrate how to share a description with others.

4. Collect the coats of arms, and after a day or two, randomly select five or six to share with the class. Have students guess who created each coat of arms.

FOLLOW-UP

Have students write paragraphs in response to this question: What did you learn about yourself as you completed the activity?

HANDS-ON HEALTH
Activity 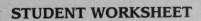 **7**

My Coat of Arms

Directions: Follow these steps to fill in each numbered area in your coat of arms.

1. Draw a picture to represent one thing you do very well. In the smaller space, draw a picture to represent something you are trying to improve.

2. Draw a picture that represents a value to which you are deeply committed.

3. Draw a picture of a material possession that is especially important to you.

4. Draw a picture to represent your greatest achievement in the past year. In the smaller space, draw a picture to represent your greatest setback.

5. Draw a picture to represent one of your important long-term goals.

6. Write three positive words that describe your personality.

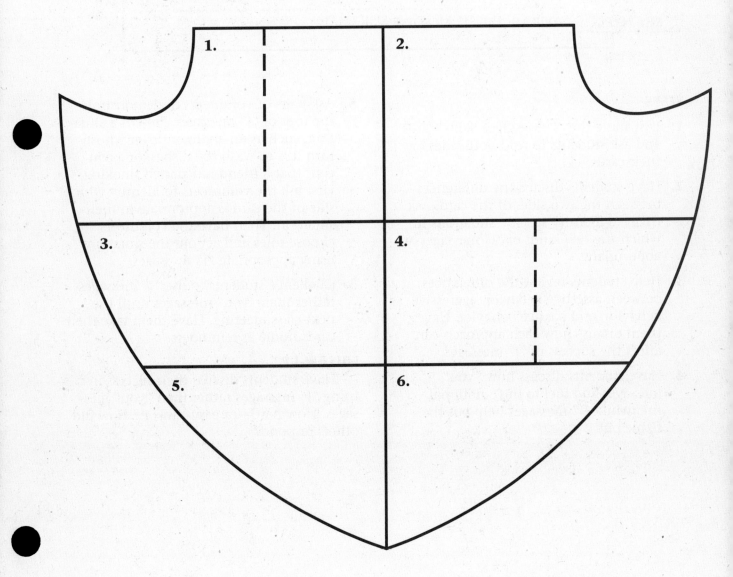

Using "I" Messages

OBJECTIVE   To practice using "I" messages and to understand the importance of this form of communication

TEACHER NOTES   Students can use this form of communication to help those they care about confront such difficult problems as drug or alcohol use, sexual activity, suicidal thoughts, and eating disorders. Using the metaphor of a campfire, explain how negative messages are like adding logs to an already large fire. The "I" messages represent the rain. Rain puts out the fire, and using "I" messages defuses or eliminates the conflict.

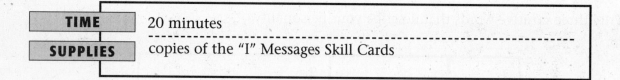

TIME	20 minutes
SUPPLIES	copies of the "I" Messages Skill Cards

STEPS

1. Distribute the "I" Messages Skills Cards and ask students to read both sides of their cards.

2. Have students discuss the differences between the two sides of the card. Ask them to identify specific situations in which the two kinds of "I" messages are appropriate.

3. Help students review the differences between assertive behavior, aggressive behavior, and passive behavior. Have them discuss how each approach can affect the success of "I" messages.

4. Have students discuss how "you" messages add fuel to the emotional fire, while "I" messages help put the flame out.

5. Ask pairs of volunteers to demonstrate the uses of "I" messages. Present a situation, such as an argument over whose turn it is to wash the dishes, or a concern that a friend has started smoking. First ask the volunteers to identify which side of the card is appropriate to their situation. Then have the volunteers choose roles and act out the situation, using appropriate "I" messages.

6. Challenge students to use "I" messages rather than "you" messages until the next class meeting. Have them take their cards home as reminders.

FOLLOW-UP

Have students discuss their success in using "I" messages rather than "you" messages. How hard—or easy—was it? How did others respond?

"I" Messages Skills Cards

Teacher Directions: Make two-sided copies, with one side reproducing "handling conflict" statements, and the other side reproducing "sharing concern" statements. Then cut along the solid lines to make individual cards, one for each student.

HANDLING CONFLICT
Use these sentences to help another person understand your feelings and to help establish a compromise.

I feel _____
when _____
because _____
I'd like/I want _____
Would you consider _____ ?

HANDLING CONFLICT
Use these sentences to help another person understand your feelings and to help establish a compromise.

I feel _____
when _____
because _____
I'd like/I want _____
Would you consider _____ ?

HANDLING CONFLICT
Use these sentences to help another person understand your feelings and to help establish a compromise.

I feel _____
when _____
because _____
I'd like/I want _____
Would you consider _____ ?

HANDLING CONFLICT
Use these sentences to help another person understand your feelings and to help establish a compromise.

I feel _____
when _____
because _____
I'd like/I want _____
Would you consider _____ ?

HANDLING CONFLICT
Use these sentences to help another person understand your feelings and to help establish a compromise.

I feel _____
when _____
because _____
I'd like/I want _____
Would you consider _____ ?

HANDLING CONFLICT
Use these sentences to help another person understand your feelings and to help establish a compromise.

I feel _____
when _____
because _____
I'd like/I want _____
Would you consider _____ ?

"I" Messages Skills Cards

SHARING CONCERN

Let someone know that you are concerned in a nonjudgmental way. Share your own ideas and feelings.

I care about/love _____

I see/I feel _____

(Actively listen to the other person)

I'd like/I want _____

I will _____

SHARING CONCERN

Let someone know that you are concerned in a nonjudgmental way. Share your own ideas and feelings.

I care about/love _____

I see/I feel _____

(Actively listen to the other person)

I'd like/I want _____

I will _____

SHARING CONCERN

Let someone know that you are concerned in a nonjudgmental way. Share your own ideas and feelings.

I care about/love _____

I see/I feel _____

(Actively listen to the other person)

I'd like/I want _____

I will _____

SHARING CONCERN

Let someone know that you are concerned in a nonjudgmental way. Share your own ideas and feelings.

I care about/love _____

I see/I feel _____

(Actively listen to the other person)

I'd like/I want _____

I will _____

SHARING CONCERN

Let someone know that you are concerned in a nonjudgmental way. Share your own ideas and feelings.

I care about/love _____

I see/I feel _____

(Actively listen to the other person)

I'd like/I want _____

I will _____

SHARING CONCERN

Let someone know that you are concerned in a nonjudgmental way. Share your own ideas and feelings.

I care about/love _____

I see/I feel _____

(Actively listen to the other person)

I'd like/I want _____

I will _____

Pat on the Back

OBJECTIVE   To share sincere, positive comments with peers and to respond to positive comments

TEACHER NOTES This activity is especially useful for bolstering students' self-esteem and for developing a positive classroom environment. You may choose to participate with students, giving and receiving written compliments.

TIME	30 minutes
SUPPLIES	• tape or CD player, song with a positive message • copies of Activity 9 worksheet, "Pat on the Back," one for each student • pen or pencil for each student

STEPS

1. Distribute copies of the worksheet and have students write their own name in the center of the palm.

2. Tell students that when you turn on the music, they should get up out of their chairs and walk around the room. Explain that they are to look for a classmate's worksheet that has an empty finger and write a sincere, honest compliment on that finger and sign their name to the compliment.

3. After each student signs one pat-on-the-back finger, have all students move quickly to the worksheet of another classmate and do the same thing.

4. The students have until the song is over to write on as many worksheets as possible, sharing honest and sincere compliments with their peers. Every person should have a minimum of five compliments!

5. When a person has five compliments, be sure to turn the paper over so it is not viewed by anyone, including the owner of the paper.

6. When the music is done, students are to go back to their desks, turn their papers over, and read and reread the compliments that their peers wrote about them.

7. Have students complete the sentences at the bottom of their own worksheets. Ask for volunteers to share the impact that this activity had on them.

8. Collect the worksheets to assess that the students did indeed give and receive honest and sincere compliments. (Collecting worksheets will make students accountable for doing the activity properly!)

9. Share with the students that for every "put-down" you make of another person, it can take as many as ten or more compliments to ease the pain of that one negative comment!

FOLLOW-UP
Challenge students to compliment people whom they often ignore, avoid, or even criticize. Remind students that these must be honest compliments, sincerely delivered. Later, let students discuss how others responded to their unexpected compliments.

HANDS-ON HEALTH
Activity ⑨   **STUDENT WORKSHEET**

Pat on the Back

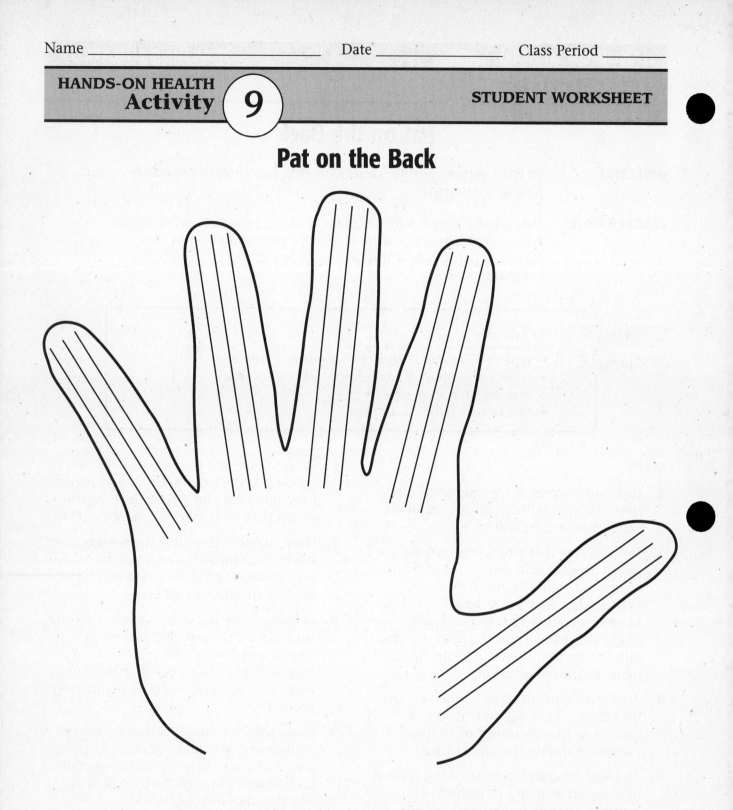

After you have read the comments others wrote on this worksheet, finish these sentences.

I feel _____

I feel _____

I feel _____

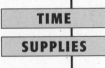

Breaking the Cycle

OBJECTIVE   To identify characteristics of healthy and unhealthy relationships

TEACHER NOTES   Identifying the differences between healthy and unhealthy relationships is one of the first steps in breaking the cycle of abuse.

TIME   30–40 minutes

SUPPLIES
- copies of Activity 10 worksheet, "Relationships T-Chart," one for every two or three students
- pen or pencil for each student

STEPS

1. Have students identify familiar couples from current movies, TV shows, and books. Ask students to recall specific words and actions that show how the two people in each couple communicate and treat each other. Examples: *Suzanne makes negative comments about Ken, both to his face and behind his back. Leroy encourages Jayne to finish school so she can get the job she wants.* List these behaviors on the board.

2. Have students form cooperative groups of two or three. Give each group a copy of the worksheet. Ask group members to discuss the behaviors listed on the board and decide whether each is characteristic of a healthy relationship or an unhealthy relationship. When they agree, have them record the behavior in the appropriate column of the chart.

3. Ask group members to recall and discuss other behaviors they may have observed between members of couples they know. Have them decide whether these additional behaviors indicate characteristics of a healthy or unhealthy relationship. Instruct the group members to record those behaviors on their chart, too.

4. In a class discussion, have groups compare their assessment of indicators of healthy and unhealthy relationships.

5. Guide students in discussing why people stay in unhealthy relationships. Focus the discussion by asking: What are the essential differences between healthy and unhealthy relationships? What constitutes abuse? Why do people stay in abusive relationships? In what senses do abusive relationships form a cycle? What skills do people need to break the cycle of abuse?

6. Based on what they have learned, have students write a statement that describes the elements of a healthy relationship.

7. Discuss students' statements. On the board generate a classroom definition of a healthy relationship that can be displayed as a banner or poster in the classroom.

FOLLOW-UP

Ask volunteers to gather information about local and national agencies that offer assistance to people in unhealthy relationships, particularly physically abusive relationships. Students may then create a wallet card or pamphlet that includes this information.

Name _____ Date _____ Class Period _____

Relationships T-Chart

Healthy Relationships	Unhealthy Relationships

Nutrition
and
Health

Cups of Calcium

OBJECTIVE   To observe the amount of calcium in the body at various ages and to recognize the importance of calcium in the diet

TEACHER NOTES   This activity can be used most effectively after students have read about the importance of calcium in the diet.

TIME	20 minutes

SUPPLIES
- 10 pounds white flour
- clear, resealable plastic bags: 1 sandwich size, 1 quart size, 3 gallon size (or 5 gallon size)
- set of measuring cups

STEPS

1. Prepare 5 cards or sheets of paper and make the following labels:

Newborn skeleton	¼ cups
10-year-old skeleton	3½ cups
15-year-old skeleton	7 cups
Adult skeleton	11 cups
Adult skeleton with osteoporosis 30–40% bone loss	6½ cups

2. Explain to students that they are going to use flour to represent the amount of calcium that should be in the bones of healthy people in various stages of life. Ask volunteers to measure flour into individual plastic bags, using the measurements noted on the labels. Display the bags of flour and their labels so that all students can see them.

3. Guide students in describing and comparing the amounts of "calcium" in the bags. Ask students to explain how a person accumulates calcium from newborn to 10 years old and then to 15 years old.

4. Ask about the differences between the amounts of calcium in the skeleton of a healthy 15-year-old and the skeleton of a healthy adult: What does that mean about the importance of a calcium-rich diet for teens? Predict what would happen if a person is 25 but has the amount of calcium of a 10-year-old because his or her diet was calcium deficient for years.

5. Emphasize that bones with sufficient calcium are strong and dense. When a person's diet does not provide enough calcium for everyday life functions (such as blood clotting and regulating heartbeat), the body takes calcium from bones. Over time, this drain can weaken bones.

6. Emphasize that the "window of opportunity" closes quickly as one grows older, and that the teen years are a very critical time to consume approximately 1200 mg of calcium daily.

FOLLOW-UP

Have students work in small groups to write their own lists of foods that are both appealing and high in calcium. In addition, have a group of volunteers research and report on the effects of caffeine on calcium and calcium absorption in the body.

Activity 12

Rubber Bones

OBJECTIVE   To observe the effects of calcium deficiency on bone strength and bone density

TEACHER NOTES   Note that the raw bones used in this activity should be washed clean and then allowed to dry thoroughly. It is best to let the bones sit out, as on a kitchen counter, for several days. If turkey bones are not available, you can use chicken bones instead.

TIME   5–10 minutes in one class session; 20 minutes in a second class session, one week later

SUPPLIES
- several cans of different types of soda
- 2 clean, dry turkey bones
- 2 clear, resealable plastic bags
- glass jar with lid
- white vinegar (about 2 cups)

STEPS

1. Display several cans of soda on a table. Ask students to read the labels, looking for caffeine, phosphoric acid, and citric acid. Discuss the effects that these ingredients have on a person's bones and have students predict what would happen to the bones of a teen who substituted soda for milk and/or drank three or four cans of soda on a daily basis.

2. Let students examine and handle the two turkey bones. Ask volunteers to describe the bones.

3. Pour the vinegar into the jar and place one of the bones in the vinegar. Twist the lid onto the jar. Place the other bone inside a plastic bag and seal the bag.

4. Explain that one bone will remain in the vinegar for a week and the other bone will be left on the counter beside it, inside a plastic bag. Ask students to speculate about what might happen to the two bones. Record their ideas, or have a volunteer take notes; save this record.

5. After one week, have students recall their ideas about how the bones might be affected. Then remove the bone from the vinegar and display it, along with the bone that has been on the counter. Put the vinegar-soaked bone inside the second plastic bag.

6. Let students examine and handle the two bones, each in its own plastic bag. Ask: How are the two bones different now? What do you think accounts for this difference?

7. Explain that the vinegar, an acid, leached the calcium out of the chicken bone. That lack of calcium makes the bone soft and rubbery.

FOLLOW-UP

Have students work in small groups to calculate how much calcium they consume in a typical day. Help them discuss how their calcium intake is likely to affect their own bone health.

Rate Your Snack Foods

OBJECTIVE   To examine the nutritional value of various snack foods

TEACHER NOTES   You may want to provide the snack foods for this activity, or you can ask students to bring in their own favorite snacks with labels.

TIME	45–60 minutes
SUPPLIES	• selection of popular snack foods, including fruit, cookies, crackers, candy bars, and chips • Nutrition Facts labels from packaged snack foods included above • nutritional information on fruits and other unpackaged foods included above

STEPS

1. Ask students about standards that can be used to rate the nutritional value of foods. Help them recognize the following as useful measures: total calories, percent of calories from fat, sugar content, salt content.

2. Display the snack foods and give students an opportunity to discuss them briefly.

3. Have volunteers come forward. Let each volunteer choose and hold one of the displayed snack foods.

4. Select one measure, such as total calories, for ranking the snack foods. Explain that the volunteers holding the snack foods should be arranged in an ordered line, with the lowest-calorie food at one end and the highest-calorie food at the other end. Have the entire class discuss and decide on the correct order. (Do not let students refer to Nutrition Facts labels on the packaged foods.)

5. When students have agreed on the order, read aloud the relevant information from the Nutrition Facts labels and the other nutritional information you have collected. Ask the volunteers to rearrange themselves as necessary to show the correct order.

6. Repeat steps 1 through 5, using other standards to rank the snack foods.

FOLLOW-UP

Encourage students to discuss what they learned from the activity. Ask: Which nutritional values surprised you? Why? How do you think this activity will affect your choice of snack foods?

Activity 14

Name That Food

OBJECTIVE   To read and discuss ingredients listings from food labels

TEACHER NOTES   You may want to vary this activity by using different foods. You can reproduce the ingredients listings from the packages of those foods or simply read them aloud to the class.

TIME   10–15 minutes

SUPPLIES
- 3 paper grocery bags, labeled 1, 2, and 3
- bag of purple-and-white licorice candy, placed inside the grocery bag labeled 1
- package of artificial sweetener, placed inside the grocery bag labeled 2
- can of tuna-based cat food, placed inside the grocery bag labeled 3
- copies of Activity 14 worksheet, "Name That Food," one for each student

STEPS

1. Explain that food labels are designed to assist consumers with making healthy food choices. Food manufacturers are required to provide nutritional information that is accurate, complete, and useful to consumers. This includes listing all ingredients by weight in their products, beginning with the one that is present in the greatest amount.

2. Discuss with students how reading food labels and ingredients lists can help people select foods that reduce the risk of disease. For example, diets high in fat and saturated fat increase the risk of heart disease and certain types of cancer. Diets with adequate fiber, vitamin A, and vitamin C tend to lower the risk of certain cancers and heart disease.

3. Distribute copies of the worksheet. Tell students that the ingredients listings on the worksheet are their clues to the foods inside the bags. They will be playing "Name That Food," and they should guess the names of the foods by

examining the list of ingredients on each bag.

4. Have students work independently or with partners to read the ingredients lists and guess the food items. Ask students to write their guesses on their worksheets.

5. Place the grocery bags in view of the students. Begin with bag 1. Ask students to guess the name of the food in the grocery bag, and then have a student volunteer take the food out of bag 1 and show it to the class (purple-and-white candy). Continue with bag 2 (artificial sweetener) and bag 3 (canned cat food). Many students will be surprised at the selections.

FOLLOW-UP

Have students discuss how they can use ingredients lists when they make food choices. What other information should they consider? Why?

Name _____ Date _____ Class Period _____

Name That Food

Directions: Read the ingredients from the following food products, and write on the lines what food you think is in the bag labeled with the number corresponding to each label.

1. sugar, corn syrup, wheat flour, molasses, caramel color, licorice extract, cornstarch, salt, artificial colors (Yellow 6), resinous glaze, anise oil, canaba wax, artificial flavors

   _____

2. corn syrup solids, partially hydrogenated vegetable oil (may contain one or more of the following oils: coconut, cottonseed, palm, palm kernel, safflower, or soybean), sodium caseinate, mono- and diglycerides (to prevent oil separation), dipotassium phosphate, artificial flavor, annato color

   _____

3. tuna, water sufficient for processing, vegetable oil, dicalcium phosphate, sodium tripolyphosphate, tricalcium phosphate, sodium chloride, vitamin A, B_1, B_6, E, and D_3 supplements, zinc sulfate, menadione, sodium bisulfide, manganous sulfate, sodium nitrite, folic acid

   _____

Fat on a Bun

OBJECTIVE To recognize the high levels of fat in popular fast foods

TEACHER NOTES You may want to check the fat content of the hamburgers or other sandwiches served at popular fast-food restaurants in the school's neighborhood. Adjust the "servings" of lard to match those specific levels; a tablespoon of lard contains about 12 grams of fat.

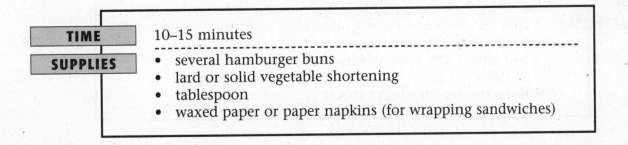

TIME	10–15 minutes

SUPPLIES
- several hamburger buns
- lard or solid vegetable shortening
- tablespoon
- waxed paper or paper napkins (for wrapping sandwiches)

STEPS

1. Let students watch as you scoop about 5 tablespoons of lard onto a hamburger bun. Spread the lard out a bit, close the bun, and wrap it in waxed paper or a napkin to suggest a fast-food hamburger. Repeat several times.

2. Offer the "lardburgers" to students, and encourage volunteers to share their reactions.

3. Ask: How are these "lardburgers" similar to the cheeseburgers and hamburgers you might buy at local fast-food restaurants? What do you think you should consider before eating those burgers? Help students recognize that the hamburgers, hot dogs, chicken, and fish sandwiches served by major fast-food chains are high in calories and especially high in fat.

4. Guide students in discussing snack and meal options other than these high-fat burgers and sandwiches.

FOLLOW-UP

Ask volunteers to gather information about the amount of calories, grams of fat, and sodium in each of 30 or more different foods served in local fast-food restaurants. This information may be found on the Internet or from the restaurants. Have these volunteers share their findings with the rest of the class. Challenge students to select a meal from each fast-food restaurant that is healthy, good to eat, and yet low in fat.

Jars of Salt

OBJECTIVE　　To recognize the amount of salt in various foods

TEACHER NOTES　　You can adapt this activity to help students recognize the amount of sugar in various processed foods. Use 1 teaspoon of sugar to represent every 5 grams of sugar listed in a Nutrition Facts label.

TIME　　20 minutes

SUPPLIES
- packages for 5 or more popular foods; Nutrition Facts should be included on the label of each package
- 5 or more clean, empty baby food jars
- container of salt
- teaspoon-size measuring spoon

STEPS

1. Display the food packages on a table or counter. Ask a volunteer or a pair of volunteers to come forward, select a package, and then find and read aloud the sodium content of a single serving of the packaged food.

2. Explain that 1500 mg of sodium is the equivalent of 1 teaspoon of salt. Have the volunteers calculate how many teaspoons of salt are included in a serving of the packaged food. Then ask those volunteers to measure out that much salt and put the salt into one of the baby food jars. Have them display the jar in front of the food package. Encourage other students to discuss their reactions to the amount of salt in that food.

3. Continue with other volunteers until the salt content of each food has been calculated and displayed.

4. Remind students that a person should consume between 500 mg and 2400 mg of salt each day—no more! Ask how eating the foods on display would affect a person's salt consumption. Also ask students how they can keep their salt intake within the healthy range.

FOLLOW-UP

Ask a group of volunteers to prepare a list of appealing low-salt snacks and meals. Interested students might also begin a file of low-salt recipes.

Substance Abuse
and
Tobacco

Tobacco Death List

OBJECTIVE   To recognize and identify some of the dangerous chemicals in tobacco products

TEACHER NOTES   You may prefer to use drawings or photographs to represent all the listed supplies for this activity.

TIME   15 minutes

SUPPLIES
- specimen in a jar of formaldehyde (formaldehyde)
- empty antifreeze bottle (propylene glycol)
- photograph of the label from a box of rat poison (cyanide, arsenic)
- photograph of an atomic bomb explosion (plutonium 20)
- photograph of a mortuary (toluene)
- set of artist's oil paints (cadmium)
- jar of rubber cement (benzene)

STEPS

1. Display the supplies listed above, and give students an opportunity to examine and discuss them. Ask: What do you think all these things have in common?

2. Help students identify the chemical each item or photograph represents. (Chemicals are named in parentheses above.) Have students share their understanding of the dangers of these chemicals.

3. Ask: Where can you find all these chemicals? Explain that they are all in cigarettes. Help students recognize that these are just some of the dangerous substances to which smokers expose themselves and the people around them.

FOLLOW-UP

Hold short group or class discussions in which students can share their reactions to this activity. How does the information about chemicals in tobacco affect their own decisions about smoking? How does it affect their responses to smoking by their peers?

Tobacco Risk Game

OBJECTIVE   To review key terms and concepts related to the use of tobacco

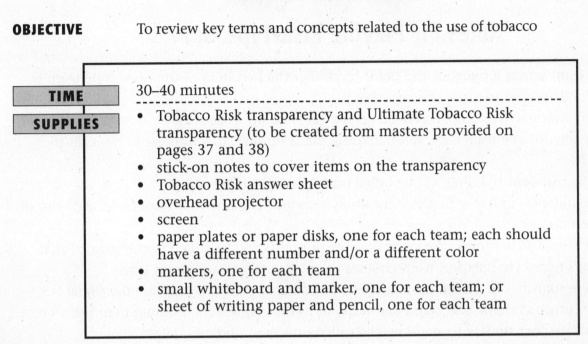

TIME   30–40 minutes

SUPPLIES
- Tobacco Risk transparency and Ultimate Tobacco Risk transparency (to be created from masters provided on pages 37 and 38)
- stick-on notes to cover items on the transparency
- Tobacco Risk answer sheet
- overhead projector
- screen
- paper plates or paper disks, one for each team; each should have a different number and/or a different color
- markers, one for each team
- small whiteboard and marker, one for each team; or sheet of writing paper and pencil, one for each team

STEPS

1. Divide the class into teams, each with three to five players.

2. Review the rules for playing this game. (page 36)

3. Display the Tobacco Risk transparency, with individual stick-on notes covering all the items. Act as the game show host and scorekeeper as students play the game.

4. At the end of the game, give each team 50 bonus points and announce the scores.

5. Review the rules for playing the last part of the game, Ultimate Tobacco Risk. (page 36)

6. Display the Ultimate Tobacco Risk transparency. Again, act as the game show host and scorekeeper as students complete the game.

7. Announce the scores and congratulate the winning team.

FOLLOW-UP

Give students an opportunity to discuss and react to the game. Which game items were most difficult? Why? Encourage students to discuss the importance of being familiar with the information on which the game is based.

Rules for Playing Risk-Type Games

- One team selects a category and point level. (For the first item of the game, one team is randomly picked to make this selection.)
- The answer for that item is revealed on the game board. (The stick-on note is removed.)
- A member of any team may stand, holding the team disk, to volunteer to respond to that item.
- The first student standing will be called on and asked to respond.
  That student—and only that student—may respond. The response must be in the form of a question.
- If the response is correct, the given number of points will be added to the score of that player's team. That player's team chooses the next category and point level.
- If the response is incorrect, no points will be added or subtracted. When the signal is given, other students may stand and respond to that same item, holding their team's disk. Again, the first student to stand will be called on to respond.
- Play continues until all the items on the game board have been revealed.

Rules for Playing Ultimate Tobacco Risk,
The Last Round of the Game

- Team members consider their total points and decide how many to risk on the Ultimate Tobacco Risk question. They record that number of points on the team disk.
- The Ultimate Tobacco Risk answer is projected.
- Teams have 60 seconds to decide on and record the correct response. (The responses may be written on whiteboards or on paper.) Responses must be in the form of a question.
- The correct response is announced. Each team shows its written response. If the response is correct, the points risked are added to the team score; if the response is incorrect, the points risked are subtracted.

Teacher Directions: You can make this into an overhead transparency by reproducing it on a clear transparency sheet in a copy machine.

Tobacco Risk Game

	10 Points	20 Points	30 Points	40 Points
Definitions	a physical or psychological dependence on a substance or activity	tobacco that is sniffed through the nose or chewed	a drug that increases the action of the central nervous system, the heart, and other organs	cancer-causing substances
Cigarettes	smoke inhaled by nonsmokers	a colorless, odorless, poisonous gas that passes through the lungs into the blood	the smoke that a smoker blows off	increased chance of spontaneous abortion and pre-natal death, low birth weight, and growth and devel-opment problems during early childhood
Diseases	the leading cause of cancer deaths among males	an inflam-mation of the bronchi in the lungs, more common among smokers than among nonsmokers	a smoking-related disease in which the alveoli in the lungs burst and blend to form fewer, larger sacs with less surface area	thickened, white, leathery-appearing spots on the inside of a smoke-less-tobacco user's mouth
Statistics	the fraction that tells how many people who begin smoking as teens will eventually die from a smoking-related cause	the number of Americans who are regular users of smokeless tobacco	the period of time after quitting smoking in which an ex-smoker's oxygen levels rise to normal	the number of American teens who light up their first cigarette every day

Teacher Directions: You can make this into an overhead transparency by reproducing it on a clear transparency sheet in a copy machine.

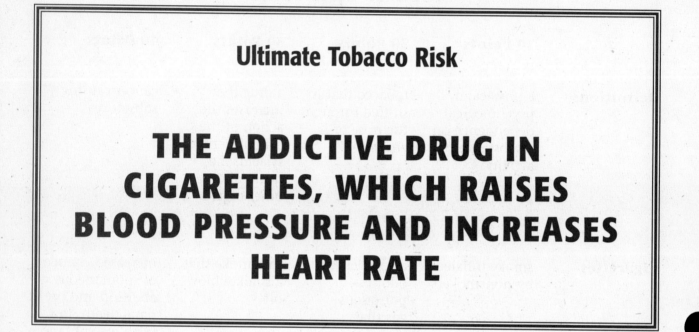

Ultimate Tobacco Risk

THE ADDICTIVE DRUG IN CIGARETTES, WHICH RAISES BLOOD PRESSURE AND INCREASES HEART RATE

Teacher Directions: You can make this into an overhead transparency by reproducing it on a clear transparency sheet in a copy machine.

Answers to Tobacco Risk Game

	10 Points	20 Points	30 Points	40 Points
Definitions	What is an addiction?	What is smoke-less tobacco?	What is a stimulant?	What are carcinogens?
Cigarettes	What is passive smoke?	What is carbon monoxide?	What is mainstream smoke?	What are some risks of smoking during pregnancy?
Diseases	What is lung cancer?	What is bronchitis?	What is emphysema?	What are leukoplakia?
Statistics	What is one-third?	What is 12 million?	What is 8 hours?	What is 6,000?

Answer to Ultimate Tobacco Risk

WHAT IS NICOTINE?

Tobacco and My Body

OBJECTIVE   To identify and discuss the health risks of using tobacco products

TEACHER NOTES   This activity can be used as a preteaching assessment or as a review activity. As an alternative to the steps below, you might have students use a black marker to outline the body and a blue marker to identify health risks. After discussing the health risks of tobacco products, return to the butcher paper and have students add to the picture using a red marker to show additional risk factors they learned about from the discussion.

TIME   30–45 minutes

SUPPLIES
- long strips of butcher paper (about 6 feet each), one for each group
- sets of colored markers, one for each group

STEPS

1. Have students form groups of three, four, or five. Distribute the strips of butcher paper and the sets of colored markers.

2. Have the members of each group spread the strip of butcher paper on the floor, and let one group member volunteer to lie down on his or her back on the paper. Ask the other group members to use markers to draw an outline of the student on the paper.

3. Then have group members discuss the effects of tobacco use on the body. As each student identifies a negative consequence or health risk that occurs due to the use of a tobacco product, other group members draw that risk on the butcher paper. For example, students might use yellow to draw affected teeth and black to draw affected lungs.

4. After groups have completed their drawings, have them show their work to the rest of the class and discuss their ideas about the effects of tobacco use.

FOLLOW-UP

Have the members of each group select and research one specific effect of tobacco use on the body. Ask groups to share their findings in oral presentations or skits.

Jar of Tar

OBJECTIVE   To recognize the dangerous amounts of tar that accumulate in the lungs of a person who smokes one pack of cigarettes a day for one year.

TEACHER NOTES   You may want to have a student volunteer prepare and present the demonstration in this activity.

TIME   10–15 minutes

SUPPLIES
- glass jar with lid
- 1 cup of dark brown corn syrup or 1 cup of dirty car oil
- packaging tape

STEPS

1. Pour the cup of corn syrup or oil into the jar, twist the lid on, and secure the lid with packaging tape to prevent leaks. Show the contents of the jar to students; explain that the dark liquid represents that amount of tar that gets into a smoker's lungs during a single year of smoking one pack of cigarettes a day.

2. Review the following facts with students:

   - Tar is a carcinogen. It causes cancer.

   - Only after the person quits smoking will the tar start to leave the lungs. It takes up to 15 years for the lungs to become fully free of the tar. However, if the person already has emphysema or lung cancer caused by tar buildup, quitting smoking will not cure the disease, which is likely to disable or kill the smoker.

   - The lungs of anyone who spends time with a smoker are also exposed to high levels of tar. This puts the non-smoker at risk for tobacco-related diseases, including emphysema and lung cancer.

   - Reduced-tar cigarettes and filtered cigarettes do not reduce the incidence of cancer among smokers. Cigarette filters do not filter out the tar or the diseases.

3. Encourage students to discuss their responses to the "tar" in the jar and the health risks it represents.

FOLLOW-UP

Discuss how the effects of chewing tobacco are different from and similar to smoking tobacco. Ask: How does smoking marijuana produce tar effects similar to or different from smoking tobacco? (Marijuana does not have a filter and therefore tar does accumulate in the lungs.) Tell students research has shown that smoking an entire marijuana joint can have the same tar effect as smoking up to 20 cigarettes.

Straws and Emphysema

OBJECTIVE   To experience the simulated effects of breathing with emphysema

TEACHER NOTES   In this activity, students experience the reduced breathing capacity associated with the disease emphysema. You may want to consider the family situations of your students; anyone with a close relative who now has emphysema or who died from the disease may find the activity upsetting. Caution students who have asthma or a respiratory illness before starting this activity.

| **TIME** | 10–15 minutes |
| **SUPPLIES** | very small drinking straws, one for each student |

STEPS

1. Have students briefly discuss the physical activities they enjoy. Examples might include dancing, bicycling, playing soccer, and so on. Ask students how their breathing capacity affects their ability to exercise and how physical exercise affects their breathing.

2. Tell students to stand and perform a physical activity, such as running in place or doing jumping jacks, for about one minute. Discuss how easy it is to do this activity with a healthy respiratory system.

3. Have students sit down again and give each student a straw. Have students put the straws in their mouths, hold their noses closed, and breathe only through the straws for one minute.

4. Then have students stand and perform a physical activity for one minute while holding their noses and breathing only through the straws.

5. After students have completed the minute of exercising, have them sit down again. Ask them to continue breathing only through the straws as long as possible.

6. Ask students to describe how they felt while their breathing was restricted. Explain that the reduction in oxygen they experienced is similar to the reduction in oxygen experienced by patients with emphysema. Help students review the causes and the effects of emphysema.

FOLLOW-UP

Emphasize how tobacco use affects the lungs, what causes emphysema, and how the disease affects patients. You may want to invite a local physician or nurse to speak to the class about emphysema and other lung diseases.

Substance Abuse
and Alcohol

Alcohol Risk Game

OBJECTIVE   To review key terms and concepts related to alcohol

TEACHER NOTES   This game follows the same format as Activity 18, "Tobacco Risk Game." You will need to create a new transparency and use the questions and answers provided for reviewing alcohol-related terms.

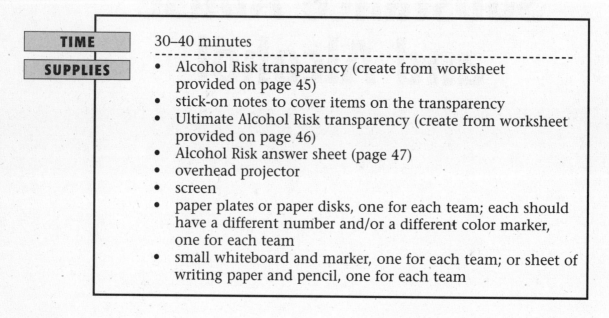

TIME   30–40 minutes

SUPPLIES
- Alcohol Risk transparency (create from worksheet provided on page 45)
- stick-on notes to cover items on the transparency
- Ultimate Alcohol Risk transparency (create from worksheet provided on page 46)
- Alcohol Risk answer sheet (page 47)
- overhead projector
- screen
- paper plates or paper disks, one for each team; each should have a different number and/or a different color marker, one for each team
- small whiteboard and marker, one for each team; or sheet of writing paper and pencil, one for each team

STEPS

1. Divide the class into teams, each with three to five players.

2. Review the rules for playing this kind of game. (page 36)

3. Display the Alcohol Risk transparency, with individual stick-on notes covering all the items. Act as the game show host and scorekeeper as students play the game.

4. At the end of play, give each team 50 bonus points and announce the scores.

5. Review the rules for playing the last part of the game, Ultimate Alcohol Risk (page 36).

6. Display the Ultimate Alcohol Risk transparency. Again, act as the game show host and scorekeeper as students complete the game.

7. Announce the scores and congratulate the winners.

FOLLOW-UP

Have students work with partners to write at least five new questions and answers that could be used in a future game of Alcohol Risk.

Activity 22

Teacher Directions: You can make this into an overhead transparency by reproducing it on a clear transparency sheet in a copy machine.

Alcohol Risk Game

	10 Points	20 Points	30 Points	40 Points
Alcohol Facts	the type of alcohol found in alcoholic beverages	periodic excessive drinking	a dangerous toxic condition that occurs when a person drinks a large amount of alcohol in a short period of time	the group of psychoactive drugs that includes alcohol
Teens and Alcohol	the age at which you can first drink alcohol without breaking the law	the leading cause of death among teens in the U.S.	a support group for people ages 12 to 20 whose parents, other family members, or friends have drinking problems	the approximate number of problem drinkers in the United States between the ages of 14 and 17
Drinking and Driving	the number of teens who are killed in the United States each day in alcohol-related motor vehicle crashes	the number of Americans who, in the past decade, have died in car crashes that resulted from alcohol use	the ratio of legally drunk drivers to the total number of drivers on the road after midnight	the percent of all teen-involved car crashes that are linked to alcohol
Effects of Alcohol	physical and mental impairment resulting from the use of alcohol	an alcohol-related condition in which fat builds up in the liver and cannot be broken down	a condition in which liver tissue is destroyed and replaced with useless scar tissue	the leading cause of mental retardation in the United States

Teacher Directions: You can make this into an overhead transparency by reproducing it on a clear transparency sheet in a copy machine.

Ultimate Alcohol Risk

THE APPROXIMATE TIME AT WHICH AN 18-YEAR-OLD CAN DRIVE HOME LEGALLY AND SAFELY AFTER DRINKING FOUR BEERS BETWEEN THE HOURS OF 11:00 P.M. AND MIDNIGHT

Teacher Directions: You can make this into an overhead transparency by reproducing it on a clear transparency sheet in a copy machine.

Answers to Alcohol Risk Game

	10 Points	**20 Points**	**30 Points**	**40 Points**
Alcohol Facts	What is ethanol?	What is binge drinking?	What is alcohol poisoning?	What are depressants?
Teens and Alcohol	What is 21?	What is driving while intoxicated?	What is Alateen?	What is 5 million?
Drinking and Driving	What is 11?	What is a quarter of a million?	What is 1:4?	What is 85%?
Effects of Alcohol	What is intoxication?	What is fatty liver?	What is cirrhosis?	What is fetal alcohol syndrome?

Answer to Ultimate Alcohol Risk

WHAT IS 8:00 A.M.?

Explanation: A teen's blood alcohol concentration must be .00 for legal driving. It takes a minimum of two hours per drink for the liver to oxidize alcohol. Since the teen had four drinks, he or she must wait eight hours.

Ranking Risk Behaviors

OBJECTIVE
To consider common alcohol-related activities teens may experience in real life, and to rank the activities according to the relative risks involved

TEACHER NOTES
You may want to revise or add to the Risk Behaviors cards, perhaps responding to suggestions from students.

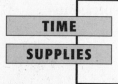

TIME   15 minutes

SUPPLIES   Risk Behaviors cards, one set for each group

STEPS

1. Divide the class into groups of four or five students, and give each group a set of Risk Behaviors cards.

2. Have members of each group work together to rank the behaviors noted on the cards, from most risky to least risky. Students should discuss their ideas about the risks involved in each behavior. If necessary, explain that group members may have to share and compare their ideas before reaching a consensus on these rankings.

3. When all the groups have completed their rankings, lead a brief class discussion about the activity: What problems did students have in ranking these behaviors? For which behaviors was it most difficult to assess the risks? Why?

FOLLOW-UP

Ask students to write short paragraphs about their group's ranking of the risk behaviors. Did group members agree or have to compromise? Are students satisfied with the final rankings? Why or why not?

Risk Behaviors

Teacher Directions: Photocopy this page, using heavy paper if possible. Then cut each sheet into seven separate cards.

Driving home after drinking two beers.

Attending a party where you know alcohol will be served.

Being driven home by a parent who hired you to baby-sit; you know this adult has been drinking.

Driving home after midnight; you have not had any alcohol.

Taking the keys of a friend who is drunk and driving the friend home; you do not have a driver's license.

Getting drunk with your boyfriend or girlfriend.

Drinking at a party and calling your sober parents for a ride home.

The Alcohol Game

OBJECTIVE To become familiar with (or to review) information related to issues of alcohol and driving

TEACHER NOTES Use this activity to introduce information to students as you begin a unit on alcohol and driving. Later, you may want to prepare cards with different questions so that students can play the game again, reviewing information they have already studied.

| **TIME** | 20–30 minutes |
| **SUPPLIES** | • 9 index cards, 5 x 7 inches
• marker
• masking tape
• chalkboard and chalk (or whiteboard and marker) |

STEPS

1. Before the activity, prepare the question cards and the game grid. On one side of each card, write a question about alcohol use and driving as well as the correct answer to that question. On the other side of each card, write a different number, 1 through 9. The following example shows both sides of one card:

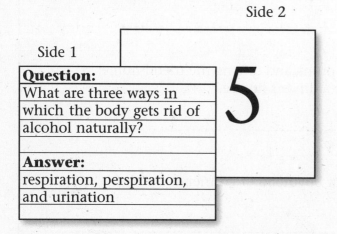

Side 2

Side 1

Question:
What are three ways in which the body gets rid of alcohol naturally?

Answer:
respiration, perspiration, and urination

5

2. Draw a large tic-tac-toe game grid on the board. Using masking tape, attach the question cards onto separate squares of the game grid, so that only the number on each card is showing.

3. Explain to students that they are going to play a game of tic-tac-toe, but they have to answer a question correctly before they can add an X or an O to the game grid. Divide the class into two teams; assign one team the symbol X and the other team the symbol O.

4. Let the two teams take turns picking a space on the game grid, identifying it by number. Remove the card with that number and ask the team the question on the card. Give the team one minute in which to answer the question, and accept only the first answer. If the team's answer is correct, write the team's symbol—X or O—in the space. If the team's answer is incorrect, return the card to the space. Either team may choose that space during another turn.

5. The game is scored just like tic-tac-toe: the first team to get three in a row wins.

FOLLOW-UP

Let pairs of students work together to make their own sets of question-and-answer cards. Then have students exchange sets of cards and play the game again.

What If . . .

OBJECTIVE   To recognize the symptoms of alcohol poisoning and to identify strategies that can help a person suffering from alcohol poisoning

TEACHER NOTES   Thousands of teens die each year as a result of alcohol poisoning. This activity helps students recognize the symptoms of alcohol poisoning and gives them an opportunity to discuss the best responses to this condition. Before you introduce this activity, you should be sure students are familiar with the effects of alcohol on various parts of the body (such as the brain, the liver, the circulatory system, and so on).

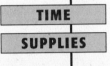

TIME   20–30 minutes

SUPPLIES   paper and pencil (or pen) for each student

STEPS

1. Read aloud the following scenario: You have been invited to a party. When you arrive, you realize that most people at the party are drinking alcohol and many are intoxicated. You decide to leave, but on your way toward the door you stumble over a person lying on the floor. This person is semiconscious, smells of alcohol, does not respond when you ask his or her name, has trouble keeping his or her eyes open, and seems to have trouble breathing. What would you do?

2. In a class discussion, ask volunteers to suggest strategies they would use to help the person in this condition. List all suggestions on the board.

3. When the list is complete, identify the strategies that will not help, and explain why each of these is not effective. For example: *Give the person coffee to drink.* This will not help. Coffee cannot help the liver work faster to oxidize the alcohol. It also presents a danger, because the drunk person might inhale the fluid.

4. Then identify the following as responses that will help:

   • Have someone call the emergency medical service (911).

   • Place the victim on his (her) side in case he (she) vomits.

   • Monitor breathing and pulse, and be prepared to do CPR.

   • If possible, find out how much the person drank.

5. Emphasize that too much alcohol can kill a person by causing breathing and heartbeat to slow down or even stop. Be sure students understand that a teen's body does not oxidize alcohol as quickly as an adult since the liver is not fully mature until a person is in their twenties.

FOLLOW-UP

Have students work in groups to brainstorm ideas for sharing information that will help others understand the extreme dangers of alcohol poisoning. (Examples include posters and public service announcements.) Then have members of each group implement their best ideas.

Disease Prevention

Are You in the Top Ten?

OBJECTIVE   To identify the top ten choices that can affect students' lifelong health

TEACHER NOTES   This activity helps students recognize the relationship between lifestyle choices and life expectancy and shows how their current lifestyle choices will enhance or endanger their health. It also gives students an opportunity to explain how they can change their lifestyle behaviors and improve their overall health. If there has been a recent suicide or similar event in your school district, be sensitive to this situation when presenting this activity.

TIME   20 minutes

SUPPLIES   • index cards, 5 x 7 inches, each labeled as follows with a cause of death, one card for each student:

Number of Cards	Cause of Death
4 cards	accidents
3 cards	homicide
2 cards	suicide
1 card	cancer
1 card	heart disease
1 card	HIV/AIDS
1 card	congenital abnormalities
1 card	pneumonia/influenza
1 card	chronic obstructive pulmonary disease
1 card	stroke
Remaining cards	old age

STEPS

1. Distribute the cards, placing them face-down on students' desks. Tell students not to turn their cards over.

2. Ask: What do you think are the top ten causes of death among teens in this country? Have students list their ideas.

3. Once students have completed their lists, let them share and discuss their ideas. Then guide students in discussing the impact that daily lifestyle choices and behaviors have on health and life expectancy.

4. Then have students turn over their cards and read the names of their "killers." Point out that those whose cause of death is old age probably made positive lifestyle choices; those with other causes of death represent victims of the ten leading causes of death among teens in the United States. Ask students to note the lifestyle choices that could have resulted in their cause of death.

(continued)

5. Read aloud each cause of death, and have students with that "killer" stand. One at a time, ask the standing students to identify the lifestyle behaviors they might have chosen that resulted in their death. For example, a student standing to represent accidents, the leading cause of death among teens, might give this response: "I died in a car crash because I chose to drink and drive at age 17."

Then ask each standing student: If you could have your teenage life back, what would you do differently? Why?

6. Follow the same procedure with each of the other causes of death.

FOLLOW-UP

Conclude the activity by asking students: Who is in charge of your health and your future? Encourage them to discuss their ideas about making positive choices and taking positive actions.

T-Chart Guessing Game

OBJECTIVE   To review the concept of communicable diseases and to identify various communicable and noncommunicable diseases

TEACHER NOTES   In this activity, students use higher-level thinking skills to ask relevant questions and to identify a concept by examining both examples and non-examples of the concept. The activity encourages students to think about what they know, and it provides a good opportunity for assessing their level of understanding.

| **TIME** | 15–20 minutes |
| **SUPPLIES** | • about 20 index cards, 5 x 7 inches
• marker
• masking tape
• chalkboard and chalk (or whiteboard and marker) |

STEPS

1. In advance, write a large, clear label on each index card. On about half the cards, write a word or phrase that identifies a communicable disease or a method by which communicable diseases can be spread. Examples: HIV/AIDS, common cold, sneezing, kissing, sharing the same drinking glass.

   On the remaining cards, write a word or phrase that identifies a noncommunicable disease or a lifestyle behavior that does not spread communicable diseases. Examples: cancer, diabetes, hugging, writing a letter, donating blood.

   Draw a large T-chart on the board. Label one column of the chart *Examples* and the other column *Non-Examples*.

2. To begin the activity, tell students that you have a concept in mind. The concept is "Communicable Diseases," but do not let the students know this. Explain that students will try to guess the concept, but only by asking questions about

the words on the cards you display. Emphasize that at no point in this activity should they state their guesses about the concept aloud or ask whether their guesses are correct.

3. As a sample, display one of the prepared cards that gives an example of the concept. Read the word or phrase aloud, tell students that it is an example of your secret concept, and tape the card in the appropriate column of the T-Chart. Explain, for example, if the concept is "freedom" students may not ask "Is the concept *freedom*?" They may instead ask: "Was Martin Luther King, Jr. an example of this concept?" Then you would answer "yes" and write "Martin Luther King, Jr." on the T-Chart under *Examples*.

4. Repeat step 3 with a prepared card that gives a non-example of the concept.

(continued)

5. Display the other prepared cards slowly, one at a time so that students can think about them and ask questions. Let students take turns asking questions about the words and phrases on those cards. For example, one student might ask, "Is the common cold an example of this concept?" and another might ask, "Is diabetes a non-example of the concept?" When the answer to a student's question is yes, tape the card involved into the correct column of the chart or write the term on the board in the correct column.

6. Continue with students' questions, developing the lists in both columns of the T-chart. Encourage students to ask questions about terms and phrases not included on the prepared cards; write students' suggestions into the correct column of the chart.

7. After the chart is about half full, ask students to raise their hands if they think they can identify the concept, but do not discuss their ideas yet. Rather, have all students write sentences defining the concept. Then continue with the guessing game.

8. When the chart is full, have students use the terms under the *Examples* column to write a definition of the concept. Have students share their definitions and what they think the concept is. Then guide students in discussing their ideas; encourage students to explain how they reached their conclusions. Finally, share with students that the concept is "Communicable Diseases."

FOLLOW-UP

Pose the following questions: How did this activity change your understanding of communicable diseases? What would you say now to help a younger student understand what communicable diseases are and how such diseases are spread? Have students write or discuss their responses to the questions.

Community
Health

Hot Line

OBJECTIVE　　To create brochures and/or cards that identify reliable sources of health facts and intervention support

TEACHER NOTES　　Students usually turn to their peers for information and advice about health issues; therefore, teens need appropriate resources for accessing accurate health facts and appropriate intervention and support skills. This activity helps students continue their health education outside the classroom and become lifelong learners.

TIME　　45 minutes or more in class, or 20 minutes in class plus out-of-class time for research and group work

SUPPLIES
- local phone books
- access to telephones
- access to the Internet (optional)
- paper, pens, markers, colored pencils, and/or other art supplies
- computer with graphics options, plus printer (optional)

STEPS

1. Read aloud an imaginary letter from a student who is in need of help. For example, the student might describe problems with drug or alcohol abuse, alcoholic parents, suicidal feelings, or trying to quit smoking.

2. Have students brainstorm a list of resources that might help the letter writer. Then have students brainstorm a list of people and agencies they would contact to help a friend with other kinds of crises.

3. Have students form small cooperative groups. Ask members of each group to work together to research, design, and produce a wallet card or brochure that will help teens access reliable health

resources. Stress the importance of listing local and regional health resources. Also encourage students to contact each agency to confirm that it is a reliable resource for teens.

FOLLOW-UP

Have the groups make copies of their wallet cards or brochures. These may be made available in the school counseling office. Encourage students to share the cards or brochures with other teens in the school and/or community.

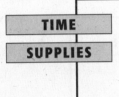
Do You Know Your Neighbor?

OBJECTIVE To take a proactive part in building a healthy community

TEACHER NOTES When you empower students to make a positive difference in and with their community, you help create growth both in the community and in the students. It is imperative that teens understand the networking needed between school, home, and neighborhood to build a healthy community. This activity provides students an opportunity to select a youth-related health issue and become proactive while working with other community members toward a common goal.

TIME 1 hour or more in class, plus out-of-class time

SUPPLIES Students will need to have access to community health professionals; specific supplies for this activity will vary according to the strategy students develop and implement.

STEPS

1. Have students brainstorm a list of health issues of concern both to teens and to the community. Examples include drinking and driving, teen pregnancy, HIV/AIDS, and violence. List students' suggestions on the board.

2. Guide students in working together to select one of these health issues as the topic for this activity.

3. Have students invite health resource professionals to visit the class for an open discussion about ways to address the selected health issue. Discussion should focus both on programs already in place and on strategies that might be developed and implemented.

4. Let the health resource professionals and students work together to develop a strategy for addressing the selected health issue and to create an action plan for implementing that strategy. (*Topic example*: drinking and driving; *Action Plan example*: assembly for all students, presented by community health professionals and health students on drinking and driving, to be held before prom.)

FOLLOW-UP

Developing and implementing an effective strategy may require a large investment of time and effort. Encourage students and provide assistance as appropriate.

You Need to Know. . .

OBJECTIVE To increase awareness of a specific teen health issue and to create a TV ad

TEACHER NOTES In this activity, students work in groups to develop, write, perform, and tape a 50-second TV commercial on a health topic of special importance to teens. You might have students imagine a local TV station has asked for ads on the theme "Alcohol Is Not for Kids." You may want to let students select their own topics. As they research, develop, and share their commercials, students will increase their own knowledge and be empowered to make a positive difference in their community.

TIME 2 hours or more in class (additional out-of-class time, optional)

SUPPLIES
- access to health resources on a specific topic, such as HIV/AIDS, skin cancer, violence, or suicide
- camera
- videotape
- VCR and monitor

STEPS

1. Have the class work in cooperative groups of three to six students each. Have groups brainstorm to select a specific teen health topic for their commercial.

2. Allow time for group members to work together to research, plan, and write their commercial. Emphasize the importance of presenting accurate, up-to-date information in these commercials.

3. Then have group members perform, film, and edit their commercial.

4. To assess the groups' commercials, create a rubric based on such factors as creativity, accuracy, educational merit, and cooperation among group members.

FOLLOW-UP

Have students work either in their separate groups or as a class to promote and distribute their commercials. For example, they might be broadcast by a local TV station, on public access TV, or during a student assembly or PTA meeting.

Human Sexuality and Abstinence

Bowl of Milk

OBJECTIVE   To identify the mixed messages teens get about sexual behavior from media, family, religious organizations, and friends, and to recognize the role hormones play in sorting out those messages

TEACHER NOTES   This activity helps students understand the mixed messages about sexuality and sexual behavior to which they are constantly exposed. It provides a way of visualizing those mixed messages and "seeing" how their own hormones make the messages even more confusing.

TIME   20–30 minutes

SUPPLIES
- large glass punch bowl
- 1 gallon whole milk (Skim or low-fat milk will not work with this activity.)
- food coloring in four different colors (blue, red, green, yellow)
- Dawn dishwashing detergent with a label "Hormones" pasted over existing label

---

STEPS

1. Pour the milk into the large glass bowl. Explain to students that the bowl represents a teenage body and the milk represents a teenage brain.

2. Ask students to identify some of the messages they get from media (radio, TV, movies, magazines) about sexual activity. Examples might include "No worries" and "It feels great." For each media message students identify, squeeze a drop of blue food coloring into the milk.

3. Next, ask students to identify messages they get from their parents and other family members about sexual activity. Examples might include "Don't even think about it" and "Nothing will happen." For each message students identify, squeeze a drop of red food coloring into the milk.

4. Follow the same procedure with messages students get from religious organizations. Use green food coloring to represent these messages.

5. Then follow the same procedure with messages students get from their friends. Use yellow food coloring to represent friends' messages.

6. When all four kinds of messages are represented by different colors, the bowl of milk will be very colorful. Ask students: How is this milk, with its multiple colors, like your brain? (conflicting sexual messages) What does this bowl of milk show about the difficulty of sorting out all the different messages you receive about sexual behavior?

(continued)

7. Finally, show students the dishwashing detergent labeled "hormones" and explain that it represents teenage hormones. Squeeze some Dawn into the middle of the bowl of milk. The milk will begin to bubble, and the colors will mix completely, so there is no possibility of distinguishing one from another. Ask: What happened to the milk? What does this show about the role hormones play in your ability to make safe, legal, healthy, and responsible decisions about sexual behavior? Predict what kinds of decisions a person might make with a mind full of conflicting messages.

FOLLOW-UP

Help students discuss how difficult it is to make healthy decisions when hormones, physical desires, sexual drive, and influences from many different sources give such mixed messages. Explain that one purpose of the unit on human sexuality in your health class is to help students sort out the messages they receive and to enable students to make healthy, legal, safe, and responsible choices, now and in the future.

Activity **32**

Who's Who?

OBJECTIVE   To review the terms associated with the male and female reproductive systems

TEACHER NOTES   This activity provides a comfortable classroom climate for students to compare the terms associated with the male and female reproductive systems and to identify the terms common to both systems. You may want to use the activity as a preteaching assessment tool before teaching the unit on reproductive systems. You could then use the activity again for review at the end of the unit.

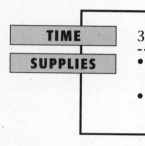

TIME   30 minutes

SUPPLIES
- Reproductive Systems Cards, one set for each pair of students (or you may use vocabulary terms from the chapter)
- envelopes, one for each pair of students (Place a complete set of Reproductive Systems Cards in each envelope.)

STEPS

1. Have students form cooperative pairs, and give each pair an envelope filled with Reproductive Systems Cards.

2. Instruct students in each pair to sit side by side as they read the terms on the cards. Have partners work together to sort the cards into three groups: terms associated with the female reproductive system, terms associated with the male reproductive system, and terms that are associated with both the female and male reproductive systems.

3. When students have placed terms in their categories, share the correct answers for each group of terms and let them correct their work if necessary.

4. Then ask students in each pair to organize the cards to show the relative positions of the organs in the female reproductive system. Have them repeat the procedure with the cards that name organs in the male reproductive system. Have students list the terms in order that the reproductive cell (ovary or sperm) travels through the system from start to end.

FOLLOW-UP

To extend the activity, have students in each pair identify similarities between specific organs in the female reproductive system and specific organs in the male reproductive system. You might present the following example: Ovaries and testes are similar because both contain reproductive sex cells.

Reproductive Systems Cards

Teacher Directions: Photocopy this page. Then cut each sheet into twenty-seven separate cards.

cervix	Cowper's gland	ejaculation
endometrium	epididymus	estrogen
fallopian tubes	labia majora	labia minora
menstruation	ova	ovaries
ovulation	penis	progesterone
prostate gland	scrotum	seminal vesicles
sperm	testes	testosterone
urethra	urinary bladder	uterus
vagina	vas deferens	sterility

Sperm Bank

OBJECTIVE   To visualize the huge number of sperm that can be ejaculated in a single act of intercourse

TEACHER NOTES   You can use this activity to help students recognize the risks of pregnancy and to emphasize the importance of abstinence.

TIME	10 minutes
SUPPLIES	• ream of unlined paper (500 sheets) • Sperm Dots page (see page 69) • three-hole punch • three-ring binder

STEPS

1. To prepare, photocopy the Sperm Dots page onto all 500 sheets of paper. (You may copy the Sperm Dots onto one or both sides of each sheet.) Punch three holes into each sheet, and place all 500 sheets inside the ring binder.

2. Show the open binder to the class, flipping through the pages. As you do so, explain these facts:

   Every dot represents one sperm.

   Each row includes 10 dots, to represent 10 sperm.

   Each page has 2,000 dots, to represent 2,000 sperm.

   The complete binder has 1,000,000 dots to represent 1,000,000 sperm (2,000,000 if you have photocopied onto both sides of each page).

   It would take 700 binders just like this to represent the 300,000,000 to 700,000,000 sperm that can be ejaculated during a single act of intercourse (350 binders if you have photocopied on both sides of each page). Ask students: How many sperm does it take to make a baby?

3. Encourage students to examine the binder and discuss their responses.

FOLLOW-UP

Have students work in cooperative groups to brainstorm other methods of helping teens visualize the vast number of sperm that can be ejaculated in a single act of intercourse.

The $250,000 Question

OBJECTIVE   To recognize that sexual behavior is controllable and that abstinence is an important tool when choosing healthy sexual behaviors

TEACHER NOTES   This activity is designed to help students recognize that everyone is capable of "putting on the brakes" when things get "too hot" sexually. It uses mental imagery to help students identify conditions in which teens face high risks of making unhealthy choices. You may want to combine this activity with Activity 36, "The Dice Game," which demonstrates the high risks of teen pregnancy and of contracting an STD.

TIME   20 minutes

SUPPLIES
- one copy of The $250,000 Question Script
- CD player and CD with soft, romantic music
- scented candle and matches

STEPS

1. Begin this activity with a brief class discussion of sexual drive, sexual behavior, and sexual responsibility.

2. Then ask students to sit quietly at their desks with their eyes closed, and to imagine the scenes you are about to describe. Read aloud The $250,000 Question Script, performing the actions indicated in the script.

3. After reading the entire script, ask students these questions:

   How many of you could put your clothes back on for $250,000? (Note that most students will raise their hands.)

Why did I choose the sum of $250,000? (Help students recognize that the sum represents the cost of raising a child from infancy through college and/or equals the cost of medical treatment for a person who contracts HIV/AIDS.)

4. Ask students to identify the factors that led to unhealthy choices in this scenario. When and how could those choices have been changed? Also guide students in discussing the implications of the episode: *Sexual behavior is controllable.*

FOLLOW-UP
Ask students to write paragraphs describing their reactions to this activity.

The $250,000 Question Script

I want you to imagine that I have asked you to house-sit my beautiful home on the riverfront for the weekend. As I drive away, you decide to call your girlfriend or boyfriend, the person you really like being with. Imagine what that person looks like. Imagine how that person smells and how you feel when the two of you are together.

Your boyfriend or girlfriend arrives, and the two of you are alone together in the beautiful house. You turn on some soft music and light a candle to create a romantic mood. Then you sit down together on the couch.

ACTION: *Turn on the music in the CD player. Light the candle.*

A small, warm fire is burning in the fireplace, and snow is falling softly outside. Life is good; you are feeling great. As the two of you snuggle closer on the couch, your emotions start to churn. The two of you kiss and hug and touch, and the wonderful feelings just grow stronger.

The snow continues to fall and the fire crackles in the fireplace. The soft music and flickering candle continue to weave their magic. The two of you go on kissing and hugging and touching, and before long the clothes start to come off—first the shoes, then shirts...

As you continue to touch and get excited, a small voice comes into your head. "We didn't talk about birth control or protection!" this voice says. "I don't have anything to use, and I don't think my partner does, either. I don't want to face a pregnancy or an STD!"

Another voice in your head answers back. "Shut up!" says this second voice. "Nothing will happen! Nothing ever happens the first time! Besides, it feels right. You couldn't stop now, even if you wanted to!"

So you continue to kiss and hug and touch. Again, you hear the two voices. "Stop and think about this," says one. "Be quiet and enjoy it," answers the other. You turn the voices off and continue concentrating on your partner and your own overwhelming feelings.

You both have reached that moment just before you lose control when you hear something. It's the front door!

ACTION: *Open the classroom door and let it close noisily.*

I have come back to the house to get my cell phone, which I had left in the living room. I walk in and find the two of you with your arms around each other! We all freeze for a moment. Then I say something that surprises you: "I will give each of you $250,000, no strings attached, if you get up right now and put your clothes on."

Activity 35

How Much Does a Baby Cost?

OBJECTIVE   To estimate, calculate, and recognize the financial costs of having a baby and raising that baby for one year

TEACHER NOTES   The cost of having and raising a baby varies according to time and place. A recent estimated total in the Midwest was about $18,000 for a baby's birth and first year of life. Before students undertake this activity, you may want to research and total current costs in your community.

TIME   20–30 minutes

SUPPLIES
- paper and pencils for each pair or group of students
- copies of Activity 35 worksheet, one for each pair or group of students
- folders containing pages from catalogs for infant furniture, clothes, toys; medical bills for obstetricians, hospitals, pediatricians, and cost of medical insurance—one folder for each pair or group of students

STEPS

1. Have students work with partners or in small groups, with at least one male and one female in each group. Explain that they will calculate how much money they will need because they are about to be given an infant to take care of for a year. They have to figure out how much money they will need to pay for the baby's birth and for raising the baby during its first year of life.

2. Ask partners or group members to work together to list all the expenses they think they will face during this year-long project.

3. When all the groups have completed their lists, distribute copies of the worksheet. Have students compare their own lists with the items on the worksheet: What did they forget? What possibly unnecessary items did they include?

4. Then distribute the folders and have partners or group members work

cooperatively to fill in the worksheet, calculating the cost of raising a baby for one year.

5. In a class discussion, have students compare and discuss the costs they calculated. (You may want to share the costs you calculated.) Ask students how their initial "guesstimates" differ from their final calculations.

6. With students, discuss how difficult it is for teens to earn the money necessary for raising a baby. Emphasize that 80 percent of those who become teen parents live in poverty five years after the birth of their first child.

7. Help students recognize that birth control is much cheaper than raising a baby. Saying NO doesn't cost a thing!

FOLLOW-UP

Have students write letters of advice to teens who are considering whether they should risk becoming pregnant.

How Much Does a Baby Cost?

Directions: First, record your "guesstimate" of the cost of raising a baby from its birth to its first birthday: _____

Use the information in your folder to determine the cost of each of these items. Then add up the separate costs to find the total cost of raising a baby from its birth to its first birthday.

Hospital Cost: _____

Shots/Doctor Visits: _____

Formula: _____

Bottles: _____

Nipples: _____

Baby Food: _____

Diapers: _____

Clothes (T-shirts, sleepers, outfits, coats, hats, etc.)

    Newborn Size: _____

    3-Month Size: _____

    6-Month Size: _____

    9-Month Size: _____

    12-Month Size: _____

Crib: _____

Mattress: _____

Sheets/Blankets: _____

Shoes: _____

High Chair: _____

Playpen: _____

Toys: _____

Car Seat(s): _____

Insurance (life insurance, health insurance): _____

Diaper Bag: _____

Toiletries (shampoo, oil, lotion, thermometer, comb, etc.): _____

Child Care (40 hours/week for 50 weeks): _____

Additional Items _____

Stroller: _____

Bumper Pads: _____

Walker: _____

Swing: _____

_____: _____

_____: _____

TOTAL: _____

The Dice Game

OBJECTIVE　　To recognize the pregnancy and STD risks of sexual activity and to understand the positive and negative effects that peer pressure can have on decision making

TEACHER NOTES　　This activity is especially useful in reinforcing the concept that abstinence before marriage is the safest and healthiest choice for teens. The activity helps students understand the risks they take if they choose to be sexually active. It also lets them recognize the role that peer pressure can play in making choices about sexual activity.

TIME	30 minutes
SUPPLIES	• dice, one for each student • small plastic or paper cups, one for each student • paper for each student • Health Bonus Bucks (page xi)

STEPS

1. Put one die in each cup, and give a cup with a die to each student. Instruct students to roll the dice from the cups onto their desks six times and to record the number they roll each time. Then have students put their cups and dice aside.

2. Review with students the consequences of the choices teens make about sexual activity. What are the likely consequences of choosing to have sex? What are the expected consequences of choosing to abstain?

3. Then have students review the six numbers they rolled and recorded. Explain that each roll of the dice represents an incidence of sexual activity. Further explain that every time a person has unprotected sex, that person faces a 1:6 chance of pregnancy.

4. Ask all students who rolled at least one 6 to stand. Tell these students that they just got pregnant or just got a girl pregnant. Ask these students to share their feelings about becoming teen parents.

5. After that set of students has been seated, ask whether any students rolled a 6 the first time. Have these students stand. Ask them to tell how they feel about getting pregnant the first time they had sex. Ask the class: Can this really happen?

6. After that set of students has been seated, ask students who rolled more than one 6 to stand. Let these students share their responses to being teen parents of more than one child.

7. Remind students that every time a person has unprotected sex, that person faces a greater chance of contracting an STD. Ask all the students who rolled one 5 to stand. Tell these students that they have just contracted an STD. Remind students that three types of STDs cannot be cured and one STD can kill them! Ask these students to share their feelings about having STDs.

(continued)

8. Ask students who rolled a 5 the first time to stand. Let these students tell how they feel about contracting an STD the first time they had sex.

9. Next ask students who rolled more than one 5 to stand. How do these students feel about having more than one STD?

10. Then ask: Is there anyone here who rolled the die six times and never got a 5 or a 6? If there is, ask whether that student wants to take a chance and roll again. If the student decides to roll again and does not roll a 5 or a 6, offer the student two Bonus Bucks to roll again. If the student continues to take the risk, continue until the student rolls a 5 or a 6. Then the student loses! Other members of the class are likely to urge the student to take the risk and keep rolling the die. Encourage these interactions. Once the student has lost (by rolling a 5 or a 6), help students recognize and discuss the impact of this peer pressure. Point out that the classmates risk nothing and the student rolling the die eventually loses, just as the teen who continues to be sexually active eventually loses by causing a pregnancy or contracting an STD.

FOLLOW-UP

Have students work in groups to design and make posters that communicate the message of this activity.

Sexy Label

OBJECTIVE   To review vocabulary related to human sexuality and to be comfortable using that vocabulary with peers

TEACHER NOTES   This activity raises students' comfort level in using vocabulary related to human sexuality. The ability to use key vocabulary terms with peers is a necessary step toward becoming sexually responsible and toward understanding human growth and development. The activity also helps students identify which concepts they know and which they need to study further. In addition, the activity enables students to use the critical thinking skills of comparing and contrasting as they ask questions to determine which vocabulary terms are on their hidden cards.

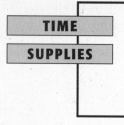

TIME   30 minutes

SUPPLIES
- index cards, 5 x 7 inches, one for each student
- markers: blue, red, purple, green, and black
- Health Bonus Bucks (page xi)

STEPS

1. In advance, prepare the cards. Write two vocabulary terms on each card. The first word should be a male anatomy term (written in blue), a female anatomy term (written in red), a pregnancy term (written in purple), or the name of a sexually transmitted disease (written in green). The second vocabulary term on each card should name a contraceptive method (written in black). Here are two sample cards:

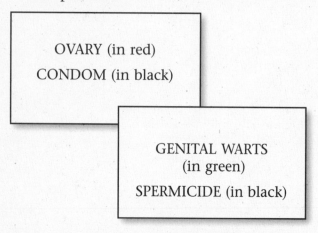

OVARY (in red)

CONDOM (in black)

GENITAL WARTS (in green)

SPERMICIDE (in black)

Also write the following key to color coding on the board (or, if you prefer, on an overhead transparency).

Blue:	Male Anatomy Term
Red:	Female Anatomy Term
Purple:	Pregnancy Term
Green:	Name of a Sexually Transmitted Disease

2. To begin the activity, have students pair up into teams of two. Give each team two cards, one for each student. Avoid letting students see one another's cards; they should not know which vocabulary terms are on their partner's card.

3. Explain that students each have two vocabulary terms on their cards. The first term is color-coded; point out the key to these colors on the board (or on the overhead transparency). Challenge students to take turns identifying the first term on their partner's card, following these rules:

- Ask your partner questions about the term. He or she may answer your questions with one of three responses: "Yes," "No," or "I have no idea!"

- You may ask no more than 10 questions in all. Therefore, you should take time to analyze each answer your teammate gives you and then give careful thought to your next questions.

4. Once students have identified the first term on their cards, have them switch roles and follow the same rules to identify the first term on the other person's card. Then switch again to identify the second terms on each card.

5. Instruct teams who have identified all four vocabulary terms to come and get a Health Bonus Buck for each team member.

6. Have students take their cards to their desks and write sentences that use both vocabulary terms, showing an understanding of the definition of each term. Here are two examples:

Each month the <u>ovary</u> in the female releases an ovum that can become fertilized during sexual intercourse if the couple chooses not to use a <u>condom</u>.

Use of a <u>spermicide</u> cannot prevent the spread of the virus that causes <u>genital warts</u>.

7. When all students have identified their terms and written a sentence, call on volunteers to read their sentences to the rest of the class.

FOLLOW-UP

Have students recall and list the vocabulary terms about which they had to answer "I have no idea!" Suggest that students look up and study the definitions of those terms.

Sex-O

OBJECTIVE   To review and reinforce understanding of previously learned terms relating to human sexuality

TEACHER NOTES   This activity is a variation of the familiar game Bingo. In order to play, students have to select human sexuality terms that they think they should know for an exam. The game requires students to be familiar with each term, knowing how to spell it and recognizing its definition. Playing Sex-O provides an opportunity for students to review important information, identify terms they should study before an exam, and have fun creating and playing the game.

TIME	20–30 minutes
SUPPLIES	• Sex-O Game Card worksheets, one for each student • students' health texts and notebooks • list of vocabulary terms that students should know for their exam on human sexuality; definitions of these terms (If possible, prepare this list of terms and definitions on an overhead transparency.) • Health Bonus Bucks (page xi)

STEPS

1. Give each student a Sex-O Game Card worksheet. Have students select 24 important vocabulary terms from their study of human sexuality and write each term in one of the empty boxes of the Game Card. They may write these words in any order they choose. Encourage students to refer to their textbooks and their notes as they select appropriate terms; you may also want to have them discuss their ideas for important terms with partners or in small groups.

2. When all students have filled in their Game Cards, the game begins. One at a time, read aloud the definitions from your prepared list. (Do not read the terms aloud.) Have students look on their own Game Cards for the term you defined. If the term is there, have students draw an X through that term, filling the entire box. Check off the term on your own list to keep a record of the words already used. (If your list is on an overhead transparency, keep the projector turned off so that students cannot read either the terms or the definitions.)

3. The players' goal is to get five X's in a row vertically, horizontally, or diagonally. Any player who achieves that goal should shout out "Sex-O." (You will have to read aloud at least four definitions before any player can achieve that goal; it may take many more definitions before a player gets five X's in a row.)

(continued)

4. To check a player's Sex-O card, read aloud the terms and their definitions, using your checkmarks as a guide. (If your list is on a transparency, project only the words you have already defined as part of the game.) Have all students check their Sex-O Game Cards. Allow them to correct their markings, erasing or adding X's to their cards. Also encourage them to list the words they defined incorrectly. If the player who called "Sex-O" does have five correct X's in a row, award that player a Health Bonus Buck.

5. Have all students continue playing Sex-O. It is not necessary for them to begin with new cards; simply continue reading definitions from your list and having students add X's to their cards. It is possible for many students to get five X's in a row and for some students to get more than one row of X's. Check and reward each Sex-O, again reminding students to correct their own cards and to list terms they marked incorrectly.

6. Continue the game as long as you like or as long as time permits.

FOLLOW-UP

Remind students to spend extra time reviewing the vocabulary terms with which they had trouble while playing Sex-O.

Sex-O Game Card

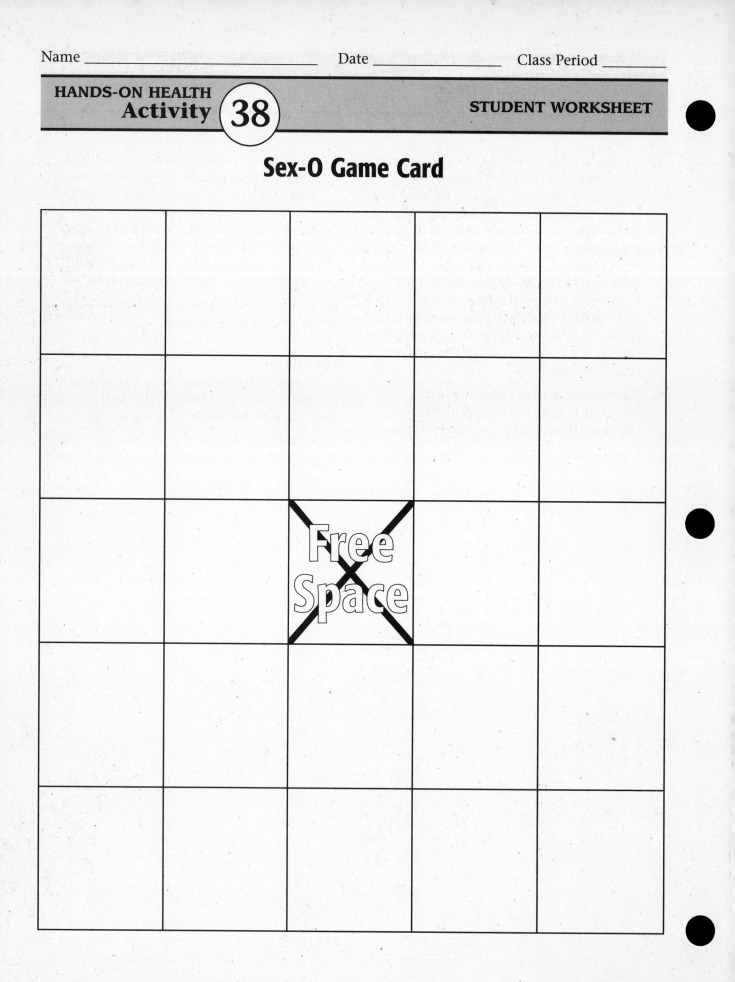

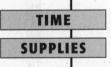

Activity 39

Sexual Health Contract

OBJECTIVE   To allow students to commit publicly that they will make healthy, safe, legal, and responsible decisions about their own sexual behavior

TEACHER NOTES   This activity can be most effectively used at the close of a unit on abstinence or a unit on STDs and HIV/AIDS. It helps students become aware of the impact that their sexual decisions can have on their own health and future lives. The activity gives students an opportunity to make a commitment to themselves, to their friends, and to their parents that they will make healthy decisions about sexual behavior, and thus avoid the negative impact that sexual activity before marriage can have on their lives.

| **TIME** | 10 minutes (more if a panel discussion is included) |
| **SUPPLIES** | Sexual Health Contracts, one for each student |

STEPS

1. Begin this activity with a panel discussion. Invite a group of individuals who have been infected with or affected by HIV/AIDS or a group of teen parents to speak to the class.

2. Distribute copies of the Sexual Health Contract. Ask students to read, complete, and sign the contract. Then encourage them to have a friend and a parent sign the contract as well. You may want to give extra credit to students who include a parent's signature on their contracts.

FOLLOW-UP

Have students discuss the impact that this Sexual Health Contract may have on the choices they make in the future. How will the public nature of the contract affect their decision-making processes?

Sexual Health Contract

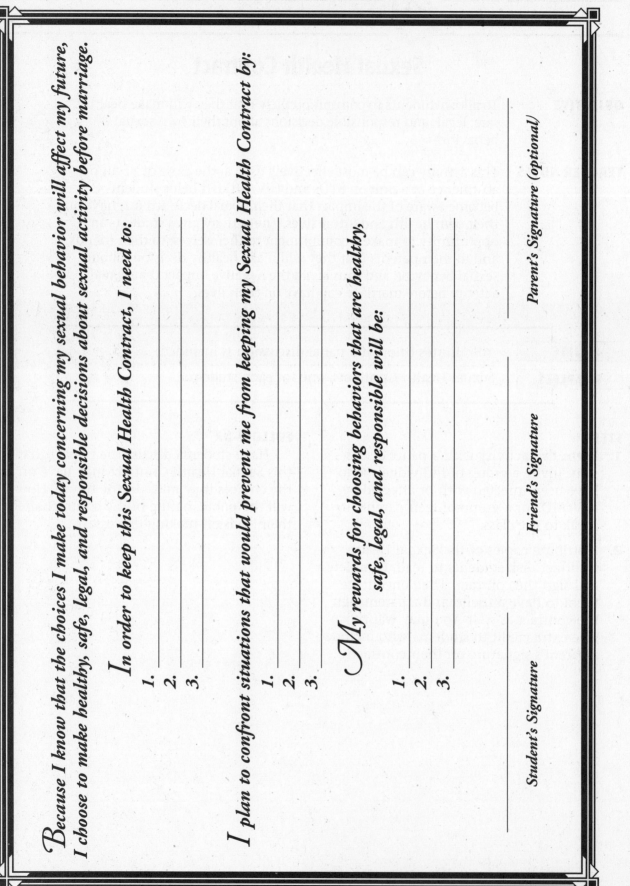

Because I know that the choices I make today concerning my sexual behavior will affect my future, I choose to make healthy, safe, legal, and responsible decisions about sexual activity before marriage.

In order to keep this Sexual Health Contract, I need to:

1. _____
2. _____
3. _____

I plan to confront situations that would prevent me from keeping my Sexual Health Contract by:

1. _____
2. _____
3. _____

My rewards for choosing behaviors that are healthy, safe, legal, and responsible will be:

1. _____
2. _____
3. _____

_____
Student's Signature

_____
Friend's Signature

_____
Parent's Signature (optional)

STDs, HIV, and AIDS

Candlelight Ceremony

OBJECTIVE   To understand the devastation that HIV/AIDS has caused throughout the world

TEACHER NOTES   This activity is an abbreviated version of the many candlelight ceremonies that have been held in memory of those who have been infected with HIV. The activity is intended to help students "feel" what it must be like to lose someone—a family member, a friend, even an acquaintance—to AIDS. It is hoped that participating in the ceremony will empower students to choose healthy behaviors that will not put them at risk for contracting HIV. Be sensitive to personal experiences of students who may have been affected by HIV/AIDS.

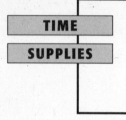

TIME   15 minutes

SUPPLIES
- pictures of the AIDS quilt
- candles, one for each student
- matches

STEPS

1. Show pictures of the AIDS quilt, and emphasize that each patch on this quilt commemorates an individual who has died of AIDS. Help students discuss why friends and relatives of AIDS victims might create a section for this quilt. What feelings do you think they hope to express by participating in the quilt project?

2. Help students discuss candlelight ceremonies they may have seen or participated in. What feelings were the ceremonies intended to express? What mood did they create?

3. Tell students that the class will be holding its own candlelight ceremony for AIDS patients and victims. Ask whether they have any specific ideas about making the ceremony meaningful, and incorporate as many of these ideas as possible. Distribute the candles, keeping one for yourself. Use a match to light your own candle, and let students come forward, one at a time, to light their candles from yours. Encourage students to share brief comments as they light their candles.

FOLLOW-UP
If possible, combine this ceremony with an in-class discussion headed by a group of community members who have been infected with or affected by HIV/AIDS.

AIDS Egg

OBJECTIVE To demonstrate how the human immunodeficiency virus (HIV) invades and infects the immune system

TEACHER NOTES The activity provides a good opportunity for assessing students' knowledge about the transmission of HIV/AIDS. Use what you learn from the students' demonstrations to tailor future lessons specifically to their current level of skill and knowledge. In addition, the activity encourages students to talk with their peers about HIV/AIDS, sharing what they know and learning more about the transmission of HIV/AIDS. Encourage students to be creative in developing their demonstrations; remind them that each demonstration should be unique.

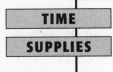

TIME 30–45 minutes

SUPPLIES
- large, hollow plastic eggs that open, one for each group
- miniature marshmallows, 15–20 for each group

STEPS

1. Have students form small groups of two or three. Distribute one plastic egg and 15 to 20 miniature marshmallows to each group.

2. Tell students that each group should plan a short presentation using the egg and the marshmallows to demonstrate how HIV infects the human body and the immune system. Remind students of the importance of working cooperatively, and set a specific time limit for planning (five to seven minutes).

3. Give students this sample demonstration: Put all but one of the marshmallows inside the egg and close it. Hold up the marshmallow in one hand and explain that it represents HIV. Hold up the egg in the other hand and explain that it represents a T cell. Then explain

that when HIV enters the T cell, it multiplies and destroys the T cell. To demonstrate, open the egg (the T cell) and show all the marshmallows (HIV) inside.

4. At the end of the planning period, have each group present its demonstration to the rest of the class. Encourage the students watching each demonstration to follow closely and ask pertinent questions. If necessary, clarify any mistaken impressions and correct any misinformation presented in the groups' demonstrations.

FOLLOW-UP

Suggest that interested students choose other materials to create additional demonstrations showing how HIV invades the human immune system.

Activity 42

HIV/STD Pyramid

OBJECTIVE   To recognize how quickly HIV/AIDS and STDs can be transmitted

TEACHER NOTES   This activity provides a vivid demonstration of how quickly STDs or HIV can be spread through large populations and shows that abstinence from sexual activity before marriage is the only choice that can fully protect an individual's health.

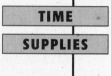

| TIME | 15–20 minutes |
| SUPPLIES | index cards, 5 x 7 inches, labeled with instructions as shown in step 1; one card for each student. Label four of these cards with a letter as indicated. |

STEPS

1. In advance, prepare cards with the following instructions:

Number of Cards	Instructions
2 cards	Shake hands with four people. A
2 cards	Shake hands with four people. G
2 cards	Don't shake hands with anyone.
2 cards	Shake hands with as many people as you can.
2 cards	Shake hands with only one person who has this same instruction.
remaining cards	Shake hands with four people.

2. Distribute the cards, placing them face-down on students' desks. Have students read their own cards without letting anyone else see them.

3. Give students two minutes in which to carry out the directions on their cards.

4. Present a prepared lesson on HIV/AIDS.

5. At the end of the lesson, read the following explanation to the class:

You know that you cannot get HIV/AIDS by shaking hands. However, for the sake of this activity, we will *pretend* that you can. Now, think back to our hand-shaking activity. Look at the card I gave you. If there is an A on your card, please stand up.

(Two students stand.) You both have AIDS. Every time you shook hands with someone, you may have infected that person with HIV/AIDS. If anyone here shook hands with these two people, please stand up.

(More students stand.) You all may be infected with HIV/AIDS. If you are infected, you may have infected anyone else with whom you shook hands. If anyone shook hands with someone who is now standing, please also stand up.

6. Continue until all but four students are standing. Let the students who are standing share their feelings about the possibility of being infected with HIV/AIDS.

(continued)

7. Then have students sit down and look at their cards again. Ask the two students with G on their cards to stand. Explain that the G means they were wearing a glove (a condom) when shaking hands. Let these students share their feelings about the level of safety provided by the glove.

8. Ask the two students who shook hands with as many people as possible to stand. Explain that their actions represent sexual promiscuity. Let them share their feelings about the health risks they face.

9. Have the two students who shook hands with only one other person to stand. Explain that their actions represent monogamy. Ask how they feel about their choices. What risks do they face when they break up their monogamous relationship?

10. Finally, have the two students who did not shake hands with anyone stand. Explain that their actions represent abstinence. Let these students share their feelings about their choice and explain how they faced the peer pressure to shake hands with other students.

FOLLOW-UP
Guide students in discussing the choices teens can make regarding abstinence, monogamy, condom use, and sexual promiscuity, especially as they relate to the transmission of HIV/AIDS.

First Aid

Pop Goes the Food

OBJECTIVE   To recognize how abdominal thrusts work to clear an obstructed airway

TEACHER NOTES   This activity helps students understand how abdominal thrusts, or the Heimlich maneuver, can clear obstructed airways. You may want to use this activity to introduce a lesson on the correct procedures for administering abdominal thrusts.

TIME   10–15 minutes

SUPPLIES
- empty plastic milk jug with a pop-on cap
- overhead transparency showing the respiratory system
- overhead projector and screen

STEPS

1. Display the transparency and discuss how the respiratory system works. Explain that food can get caught in the back of the throat; this makes breathing impossible.

2. Remind students that when we breathe, we store air in our lungs. Oxygen is transferred to the blood in the lungs and is then circulated to the rest of the body.

3. Show students the closed plastic jug and explain that the jug represents a pair of lungs. The cap on the jug represents an obstruction in the airway, such as food caught in the back of the throat. The obstruction (the cap on the jug) prevents more air from getting into the lungs (the milk jug).

4. Then explain that since there is still air left in the lungs from the last breath, we can use that air to clear the obstruction.

The air in the lungs can be squeezed and thrust up, popping the obstruction out of the way. Demonstrate this with a fast, hard thrust on the upright milk jug. The cap of the jug will fly up into the air.

5. Tell students that they have just seen how the Heimlich maneuver works. Remind students that it is important to deliver these abdominal thrusts as soon as possible. The longer one waits, the more air will have been absorbed out of the lungs and into the body, and the less air will be in the lungs to force the obstruction out of the airway.

FOLLOW-UP

Have students work in groups to plan and present brief skits showing situations in which teens can save lives by administering abdominal thrusts.

CPR Order

OBJECTIVE   To review the sequence of steps in performing CPR and in responding to obstructed airways

TEACHER NOTES   This activity helps students review the precise order of the steps in administering CPR and in clearing obstructed airways. Emphasize during this activity that CPR should be administered only by a person who has taken an approved CPR certification course.

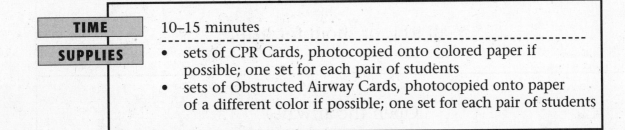

TIME	10–15 minutes
SUPPLIES	• sets of CPR Cards, photocopied onto colored paper if possible; one set for each pair of students • sets of Obstructed Airway Cards, photocopied onto paper of a different color if possible; one set for each pair of students

STEPS

1. Have each student pair up with a class-mate. Give a set of CPR Cards to each pair of students, but ask students not to look at the cards yet.

2. Explain that the cards give the nine steps in performing CPR. Students should work with their partners to read the cards and organize them to show the steps in correct chronological order. Have students wait until you say "Go." Then see which pair can finish first.

3. Check the order of students' cards, and help students discuss the correct order of the steps.

4. Repeat the same procedure with the Obstructed Airway Cards.

FOLLOW-UP

Have students work in small groups to plan effective procedures for sharing information about CPR with other teens.

CPR Cards

Teacher Directions: Photocopy this page. Then cut the steps apart to make nine strips.

CPR	Check for unresponsiveness.
CPR	Call 911, or shout for help.
CPR	Open the airway.
CPR	Check for breathing.
CPR	Give two full breaths.
CPR	Check for carotid pulse.
CPR	Position hands correctly on sternum.
CPR	Apply 15 chest compressions.
CPR	Continue to perform four cycles of CPR, and then check the pulse.

Obstructed Airway Cards

Teacher Directions: Photocopy this page. Then cut the steps apart to make nine strips.

Obstructed Airway	Ask victim whether he or she can speak.
Obstructed Airway	Perform abdominal thrusts.
Obstructed Airway	If victim becomes unconscious, place victim on his or her back and call 911.
Obstructed Airway	Check mouth for foreign body.
Obstructed Airway	Clear airway with a finger sweep. Open airway using a head-tilt/chin lift.
Obstructed Airway	Try to give the victim 2 full breaths, repositioning the head after each attempted breath.
Obstructed Airway	If breath still doesn't go in, straddle the victim.
Obstructed Airway	Give 5 abdominal thrusts.
Obstructed Airway	Repeat the sequence.

Consumer
Education

Fish Hook

OBJECTIVE
To become aware of the hidden, stereotypical sexual messages that are often used to sell products

TEACHER NOTES
This activity uses a metaphorical thinking strategy to enhance students' insights. The strategy enables learners to connect a concept with which they likely are already familiar (a fishing lure, which is a camouflaged fish hook) to a new concept (the "hooks" used by media to sell products and/or lifestyle behaviors that may be unhealthy).

TIME
20–30 minutes

SUPPLIES
- 9 fishing lures, taped to a large poster board and numbered 1 through 9
- a hundred or more magazine ads with messages that suggest sexual activity and/or drug, alcohol, or tobacco use
- slides (optional)
- slide projector and screen (optional)
- CD player
- popular music CD

STEPS

1. In advance, you will need to collect the magazine ads. You may want to have students bring examples to class. If possible, create a slide show from the ads so that all the students will be able to see the same ads at the same time. The ads should be shown in quick sequence, each for no more than three or four seconds.

2. To begin the activity, direct students' attention to the display of numbered fishing lures. Ask students to imagine that they are fish at the bottom of a lake. As they are resting, they see these nine lures pass overhead. Ask: If you were a hungry fish at the bottom of a lake, which of these nine lures would interest you most? Why?

3. Have each student write the number of the lure he or she chooses. Then have students list three or four reasons for their choices.

4. Ask students to share their answers with partners.

5. Hold a brief class discussion in which students compare and discuss their choices. On the board, list the criteria that the "fish" used to select their lures.

6. Present the slide show of ads, using the CD to provide background music. (Alternately, you can play the music while students sit in groups, passing the ads and taking quick looks at them.)

(continued)

7. At the end of the slide show or viewing of ads, ask: How are fishing lures like advertisements? Have students think about their answers and then write them down.

8. Ask students to share their ideas with partners.

9. Guide students in a group discussion of their ideas. On the board, write the metaphor findings that students suggest. Here are possible examples:

- I looked at the color of the lure, not the size of the hook!

- I may get hooked like a fish, but I take the hook off and swim away, fearing for my life.

- The ads don't tell you the whole story. The hook doesn't show the filet knife at the end of the line.

FOLLOW-UP

This activity will help students look at advertisements from a new perspective, recognizing that there is more to the story and that the hidden "hook" may have an unhealthy or even deadly side. Encourage students to share their new responses to billboard ads and radio and TV commercials.

Letter from a Fish

OBJECTIVE   To understand and use consumer rights and responsibilities; to write a letter of complaint to the Better Business Bureau about a health product that did not meet expectations or about a misleading or inappropriate advertisement

TEACHER NOTES   This activity is most effective as a follow-up to Activity 45, "Fish Hook." The activity helps students learn to confront providers of inappropriate health services and products, rather than "enabling" them by failing to complain. Students develop a skill that is essential throughout life.

TIME   30–40 minutes (or 10 minutes in class, plus out-of-class time for writing letters)

SUPPLIES
- paper and pen for each student (or access to computer and printer)
- addresses for Better Business Bureau and/or manufacturers or providers of health products and services
- business-size envelopes and postage stamps, one for each student who creates a real (rather than an imagined) complaint

STEPS

1. Help students recall the "Fish Hook" activity. Ask them to take the viewpoint of a fish who has concerns about a "hook"—a specific product, a service, or an advertisement.

2. Have students plan and write letters of complaint about real or imagined health products or services, or about ads they consider inappropriate or untrue. Remind students to follow these guidelines:

   - Use the form and punctuation of a business letter.

   - Make sure your letter is neat and grammatically correct.

   - State your complaint factually, without making threats or exaggerated statements.

   - Give specific information, including:

   - name and model of the product or service;

   - date and place of purchase or service;

   - sales receipt or service bill.

   - Explain exactly how and why you are dissatisfied with the product or service, and describe a specific response that would satisfy you as a consumer.

   - Provide information on how you can be contacted.

FOLLOW-UP

Encourage students with real complaints to mail their letters. Ask students to share the responses they receive to their letters of complaint.

What's the Hook?

OBJECTIVE   To recognize advertising techniques commonly used to "hook" consumers into buying health products they may not need

TEACHER NOTES   This activity helps students increase their awareness of ads and improve their skills in analyzing advertising techniques. This practice will help them make better, more informed decisions as health consumers.

TIME
- 15–20 minutes during one class period
- out-of-class time for finding and analyzing ads
- 10–15 minutes during a later class period

SUPPLIES
- four or more ads for health products, such as acne medicine or health insurance, or for products that threaten teens' health, such as alcohol and tobacco
- copies of Activity 47 handout, "Advertising Techniques," one for each student
- copies of Activity 47 worksheet, "What's the Hook?" five or more for each student
- audiotape and tape recorder (optional, if using radio ads)
- VCR and monitor (optional, if using TV ads)

STEPS

1. Distribute copies of the "Advertising Techniques" handout. Display and/or play selected ads from magazines, newspapers, radio, and/or TV. Guide students in identifying and discussing the advertising technique or techniques used in each ad.

2. Distribute several copies of the "What's the Hook?" worksheet to each student. Give students a few minutes to select one of the advertisements from the class discussion and complete one of the worksheets based on the discussion points. Encourage them to refer to the "Advertising Techniques" handout to provide specific information about the advertisement.

3. Have each student choose one of the following assignments:

- Select at least five health-related advertisements from one magazine. Answer the worksheet questions about each ad, and attach the ads to the back of the worksheet.

- Select a 60-minute TV program. As you watch that program, answer the worksheet questions for each advertisement.

- Select a specific health issue, such as acne, weight loss, and so on. Collect, listen to, or watch at least five advertisements that relate to that issue, and answer the worksheet questions for each ad. Attach any ads from magazines or newspapers to the back of the worksheet.

(continued)

4. After students have completed their assignments, have them meet in small groups to share and discuss their findings.

5. Ask members of each group to present their conclusions to the rest of the class.

FOLLOW-UP

Have students select two different kinds of TV programs, such as a children's cartoon show and a pro football game, or a soap opera and a news program. Ask them to compare and contrast the ads shown on the two programs. Then help them discuss factors that account for the differences between the ads on the two programs.

Name _____ Date _____ Class Period _____

Advertising Techniques

TESTIMONIAL

An authoritative person, such as a doctor, an athlete, or a movie star, testifies that he or she uses the product and you should, too. The ad may have nothing to do with the quality of the product.

SENSE APPEAL

Pictures and/or sounds are used to appeal to the senses. For example, bacon sizzles on a hot grill, or an icy beverage is poured into a frosty glass.

TRANSFER

A sexy, well-dressed, or popular person sells a product. Consumers are encouraged to imagine that they will gain those same attributes if they use the advertised product.

BANDWAGON

The ad suggests that "everyone" uses the product and consumers will be left out unless they buy it, too.

PLAIN FOLKS

An average, down-home, back-to-basics person advertises a product, encouraging the average buyer to identify with that product.

HUMOR

People tend to remember commercials that make them laugh. The humor encourages them to associate a positive feeling with the advertised product.

STATISTICS

People are usually impressed by statistics. However, many ads leave out important details about the statistics. For example: Who conducted the particular study? Who was polled? Was there a hidden agenda?

CARD STACKING

The advertisers give a one-sided view of their product, leaving out any negative aspects and concentrating only on the good features.

PUBLIC GOOD

The ad claims that its product is in the best interests of the consumer, society, or the world.

Name _____ Date _____ Class Period _____

What's the Hook?

Directions: Select an advertisement for a health product or service, and answer the following questions. If possible, attach the ad to the back of this worksheet.

1. Where did you see this advertisement? (name and date of magazine, name and date of TV show, etc.)

   _____

   _____

2. What health product or service is the ad intended to sell?

   _____

   _____

3. What "hook" (advertising techniques) does the ad use to catch your attention?

   _____

   _____

4. Do you believe that the advertised product or service will do what the ad says it will do? Why or why not?

   _____

   _____

5. To whom do you think this ad is geared? (men, women, teens, etc.) What makes you think that?

   _____

   _____

6. What other comments do you have about this ad?

   _____

   _____

Activity **48**

What Does a Body Really Need?

OBJECTIVE   To analyze techniques used to advertise health-related products and
services

TEACHER NOTES   As students participate in this activity, they will become more aware
of advertisements in popular magazines and will recognize the
impact those ads can have on consumers' choices to buy or use
particular health-related products or services.

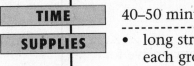

TIME   40–50 minutes

SUPPLIES
- long strips of butcher paper (about 6 feet each), one for
  each group
- markers, at least one for each group
- magazines, four or five for each group. Select different
  magazines for each group.
- scissors, at least one for each group
- tape or glue, at least one for each group

STEPS

1. Have students form groups of four or
   five. Give each group a strip of butcher
   paper, one or more markers, a set of
   magazines, one or more pairs of scissors,
   and tape or glue.

2. Have the members of each group spread
   the strip of butcher paper on the floor,
   and let one group member volunteer to
   lie down on his or her back on the
   paper. Ask the other group members to
   use markers to draw an outline of the
   student on the paper.

3. Then have group members look through
   their magazines and cut out ads for
   health-related products, both positive
   and negative. Instruct students to tape or
   glue each ad onto the body outline, on
   or near the related body part. For example, they might attach an ad for foot
   odor pads on one of the feet, an ad for
   deodorant on an underarm, and an ad
   for tobacco near the mouth or on the
   chest (lungs).

4. When groups have finished attaching
   the ads, discuss the following:

   - What health-related products
     appeared most often in your group's
     magazines?

   - To whom do you think the advertis-
     ing was directed? Why?

   - Which advertising techniques, or
     "hooks," were used most often?

   - How do you feel about the amount of
     health-related ads to which you are
     exposed every day?

   - Do you believe ads have an impact on
     a person's decision to buy specific
     products or services? Why or why not?

   - What reasons can you suggest for the
     fact that the average American spends
     more money on health-related prod-
     ucts than on medical care?

FOLLOW-UP

Ask students to design, write, and draw
original magazine ads promoting healthy
lifestyle behaviors.

Why Did I Buy This?

OBJECTIVE   To identify influences on decisions to purchase health-related products

TEACHER NOTES   This activity gives students an opportunity to examine purchases they have already made and to consider whether they really need the product, what influences their choices, and how they might respond to influences on future decisions.

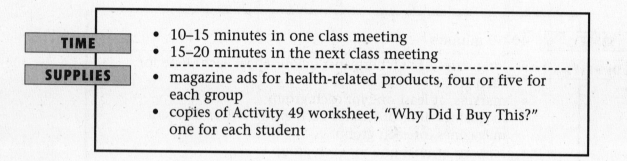

TIME
- 10–15 minutes in one class meeting
- 15–20 minutes in the next class meeting

SUPPLIES
- magazine ads for health-related products, four or five for each group
- copies of Activity 49 worksheet, "Why Did I Buy This?" one for each student

STEPS

1. Ask students to form groups of three, and give each group four or five ads for health-related products. Have the members of each group examine and discuss their ads. What advertising techniques are used? Which ads—if any—are sound, valid, and believable? How can you tell?

2. Distribute copies of the worksheet. Have students take the worksheets home and fill them in, providing information about all the health-related products they use during the next 24 hours.

3. During the next class meeting, have students share, compare, and discuss their completed worksheets.

4. Then have students imagine that they are going away for two weeks; they will have room for only five health-related products. Ask: Which five products would you select? Why did you eliminate the other products listed on your worksheet? Is it possible to reduce the number of health-related products we use daily? Do the products we choose really improve our health? Or do they just make the producing companies rich at our expense?

FOLLOW-UP

Challenge students to re-evaluate their use of health-related products and to reduce the number of products they use regularly. After two weeks, give students an opportunity to discuss the results and their reactions to this experiment.

Name _____ Date _____ Class Period _____

Why Did I Buy This?

Directions: Consider the health products you use during a 24-hour period, and fill in this chart with information about those products.

Name of Product	Where I Bought It	Where I Heard About It	Cost	Necessity?	Luxury?	Frequency of Use/Daily? Weekly?

Review the information in your chart. What seems to be the greatest influence on your purchase of health products?

Are most of the products you buy necessities or luxuries? What can you conclude from that information?

Peer to Peer

OBJECTIVE   To plan and create a poster on a specific health topic and to share that poster with a group of younger peers

TEACHER NOTES   Peer-to-peer education is one of our most powerful teaching strategies. This activity allows students to demonstrate that they have accurate information on a specific health topic and to educate younger peers about that health topic.

TIME
- 50 minutes or more (some out-of-class time)

SUPPLIES
- Travel to and from a local middle school or junior high school for presentation
- -
- large sheets of poster board, one for each group
- markers in various colors, one set for each group
- access to a group of middle school or junior high students

STEPS

1. Present a prepared lesson on a specific health topic, such as inhalants. You may also want to assign further reading on that topic.

2. During the next class meeting, help students review and discuss facts about that topic.

3. Have students meet in cooperative groups. Ask the members of each group to work together in planning and making an informative poster on the health topic the class has been studying. Explain that the posters should be designed to share the most important information on this topic with younger students.

4. To assess the groups' posters, use the rubric provided, based on such factors as creativity, accuracy, visual appeal, and cooperation among group members.

5. Arrange for students to present their posters to a class or group at a local middle school or junior high school. Students should be prepared to present and discuss their posters and to answer questions. Have students leave their posters with the younger peers as reminders of what the younger students have learned.

FOLLOW-UP

You may want to have students carry out a similar project, creating posters to share information about a teen health issue with the school board, a parent-teacher organization, the city council, or another community organization.

Health Poster Grading Rubric

Group Members: Class Period:_____

_____

_____

_____

_____

_____

_____

_____

Creativity   1   2   3   4   5
What is the message? Is it understood?

Informative   1   2   3   4   5   6   7   8   9   10
What are the Health Facts?
Are they important to know?
Do the facts persuade me not to use the product?

Attention   1   2   3   4   5
Does the poster catch my attention?

Cooperation 1   2   3   4   5
Did one person do this, or did all members demonstrate that they contributed and worked together?

Quality of Work   1   2   3   4   5   6   7   8   9   10
Is it organized, readable, artistic, neat?

Theme   1   2   3   4   5
Did the poster identify one of the following health areas? Circle which one.

Risk   Responsibility   Relationship

How did students use the theme in their poster?

Teacher's Notes

Teacher's Notes

Teacher's Notes

Teacher's Notes

Teacher's Notes

Teacher's Notes

Teacher's Notes